30-SECOND
CODING

30-SECOND
CODING

The 50 essential principles
that instruct technology, each
explained in half a minute

Editor
Mark Steadman

Contributors
Adam Juniper
Suze Shardlow
Mark Steadman

Illustrator
Nicky Ackland-Snow

IVY PRESS

First published in the UK in 2021 by
Ivy Press
An imprint of The Quarto Group
The Old Brewery, 6 Blundell Street
London N7 9BH, United Kingdom
T (0)20 7700 6700
www.QuartoKnows.com

British Library Cataloguing-in-
Publication Data
A catalogue record for this
book is available from the
British Library.

ISBN: 978-0-7112-6364-2
eISBN: 978-0-7112-6366-6

Editor **Caroline Earle**
Designer **Ginny Zeal**
Illustrator **Nicky Ackland-Snow**

Printed in China

10 9 8 7 6 5 4 3 2 1

MIX
Paper from
responsible sources
FSC® C016973
FSC
www.fsc.org

CONTENTS

INTRODUCTION
Mark Steadman

Code is one of the most significant building blocks in modern society. Every time we send an emoji to a friend, we're sending a tiny piece of code (a string of letters and numbers) across a virtual wire. That string of numbers and letters, called hexadecimal code, is then read by our friend's phone and associated with an image. When we pick up the phone to talk to our friend, code converts our analogue voice to digital data, which is encoded at one end and then decoded at the other.

What we call 'code' is a set of instructions, written in a particular language. That language depends on a number of things, like how easy it is for us humans to read and write it, how quickly a computer can understand it, the number of other computers that speak the same language and the features that language provides. Coding (or programming) can be as simple as adding two numbers together, or as complex as constructing a vast neural network that can perform complicated machine learning tasks. Code can enable mass change within a society, or it can help you rescue a few minutes from your busy day.

You don't need to have aced your maths exams in order to be a great coder. As long as you can think logically, putting one thought in front of the other, you can code. Nor do you need to memorize thousands of obscure commands, because most of us still turn to Google when we can't remember how a particular aspect of our programming language works!

You don't even need what you might consider a traditional computer in order to write code. A tablet or a smartphone will do, and there are apps that can help you learn, and achieve practical results. In this book we'll cover the key events in the evolution of computer programming, from the first-ever human computers to modern cloud infrastructures that can help scale bedroom businesses up to massive corporations.

Coding is no longer the preserve of the stereotypical basement nerd. It's everywhere, from those blocky square barcodes that we scan with our phones, to the encryption that keeps our WhatsApp conversations

COMMODORE BASIC
7167 BYTES FREE
READY.

709

```
MOVE LW-PARM-VAL TO WW-NUM-ELEMS
PERFORM B001-NEW-ARRAY

COMPUTE WW-INCREMENT =
    WW-NUM-ELEMS / 200000
END-COMPUTE

PERFORM VARYING WW-ARRAY-IDX FROM 1 BY WW-INCREMENT
    UNTIL WW-ARRAY-IDX > WW-NUM-ELEMS
    MOVE WW-ARRAY-IDX TO WW-DATA
```

```
03 LW-PARM-LEN
03 LW-PARM-VAL

PROCEDURE DIVISION USING LW-PARM.

A001-MAINLINE SECTION.

MOVE LW-PARM-VAL TO WW-NUM-ELEM
PERFORM B001-NEW-ARRAY
```

professional computer   2001 Series

from being seen by prying eyes. It's the job of these pages to open your eyes to that wider world so you can use it as you choose, whether that's to build the next TikTok or just understand why it's a good idea to turn the computer off and on again.

A tour of this book
In this book we present the ideas closest to the hearts of computer programmers (you can add your own joke about a well-known science-fiction franchise here). In academic circles, what you might know as programming is known as 'computer science', and it is a subject that isn't that old. For that reason, we've begun by devoting a whole chapter to the emergence of the computer as we understand it today, before breaking down the means by which we can instruct them. Whether it's introducing the Difference Engine or face detection, each entry is broken into several parts. The centrepiece is the **30-second code** – the explanation itself. If you're short on time, the **3-second bit** squeezes the essence of that into a single sentence, while the **3-minute byte** offers a broader context.

Computing is also more about the people involved than you likely imagined the first time you saw the blue screen of death. For that reason, this book introduces many of the names behind innovations in code and computing in general. Check out the **3-second biographies** and you'll find a little more about many of the big names past and present. The book also features more detailed profiles of some folk who you've likely heard of even beyond the geek-o-sphere!

FIRST COMPUTERS

FIRST COMPUTERS
GLOSSARY

algorithm The term for the mathematical aspect of a computer program; often an over-simplification. For example, Google is often described as having an algorithm in the singular, but many aspects go towards the system's ranking of websites.

base In maths, the base is the number on which the counting scale is based. 'Base 10' means writing numbers using ten symbols, including zero, so 0–9.

Bernoulli numbers Named for mathematician Jacob Bernoulli. He described a probability – the same each time – being calculated over repetition of the same event, for example a coin toss or dice throw.

Boolean logic In mathematics, something that is Boolean (such as the result of a certain formula) can have only two states: true or false. The term leapfrogged into computer science not just to refer to early systems but, for example, if you encounter a checkbox on a web form it'll likely be linked to an on/off or true/false field in a database.

binary Literally means composed of two things, or having two parts. In computing, a system of counting that uses base 2, and can be depicted: 0, 1, 10, 11, 100, 101, 111, 1000 and so on.

bit A bit may only have two states: on or off (usually represented as 0 or 1). The word is a portmanteau of binary digit.

DOS Disk Operating System, as opposed to DoS (denial of service – a cyber attack).

floating point A method of mathematical representation for real numbers that are especially large or small, which takes the form [significand] $\times$ [base] to the power of [exponent]: $2.5951 \times 10^4 = 25951$. You might also choose a limit on the number of digits in the significand to reduce the overall computational load on the computer – limit it to three decimal places and we would only record $2.595*10^4$ (in code * = multiply).

general-purpose computer A computer that can be programmed to carry out different operations (traditionally arithmetic or logical). Earlier devices could perform only the operation they were designed for.

loop In programming, a section of the program repeated (either until a condition is met or, by mistake, infinitely causing the program never to end).

memory The element of a computer that stores information for the active program, as opposed to 'storage'.

operating system System software that manages the computer hardware, provides common resources for applications, and allows the launching and termination of applications.

PC Personal Computer – a name coined to distinguish early PCs from the expensive room-sized computers of the time.

processor Also known as the Central Processor Unit, or CPU. This component of a digital computer performs the calculations.

program As a noun, a precise set of instructions to tell a computer what to do and how. It can also be used as a verb, meaning the act of creating a program.

punch card A card specifically designed to store information. A batch of identical cards would be printed, for example with the numbers 1 to 10 written on them. The operator could store information by punching a hole through the appropriate number. A tabulating machine could read the card from the position of the hole(s) in it.

semiconductor A material that can conduct less than a fully conductive material (such as copper) and more than insulators (such as ceramics). Silicon, an element, is a semiconductor, and (unlike metal) it becomes more conductive as its temperature increases.

silicon This is a base metal, but in computing usually refers to the components (integrated circuits) made from it, and especially central processing units, for example, 'This computer has Apple silicon'.

software A collection of data that can be read by the computer as instructions on how to work, as opposed to the hardware that actually performs the work.

statement A single line of code correctly written that makes a command.

tabulating machine The machine that processed punch cards and recorded totals or performed similar actions.

variable In programming, all data being manipulated needs to be stored in the computer's memory. A space is allocated for each piece of data and given a name so the program can access it – this is the variable.

THE INDUSTRIAL REVOLUTION

the 30-second code

When you imagine computer code, it's hard not to picture someone with questionable (or obsessive) hygiene hunched over a computer. Before we even get to the fact that this simply isn't a fair representation of the community, it's also important to realize that a concept of programming existed long before there were little glowing screens or QUERTY keyboards to complete the stereotype. In fact, the point at which humanity first began to hand over repetitive tasks to machines was the Industrial Revolution, the vanguard of which was the textile industry. In 1750, Britain imported around 1,100 tonnes of cotton, which was spun on handwheels. By the year 1800 that figure was 24,000 tonnes and growing fast. The key driving factor was the arrival of stationary steam engines powering large factories, or 'mills', processing the growing supply of cotton from the American colonies. Britain's rapid industrialization quickly made it the leading global power, which didn't go unnoticed by Napoleon. The French ruler enthusiastically supported his growing textile industry in Lyon, where Joseph-Marie Jacquard was developing his loom-related inventions. His 1801 Jacquard loom featured punch cards to weave patterned silk automatically, giving France the edge. It was made property of the French state; there were 11,000 in use in France a decade later.

3-SECOND BIT
The Industrial Revolution created the conditions for the punch-card system of data storage long before computing had been invented.

3-MINUTE BYTE
Punch cards allowed needles to pass through holes in the card, or not when no hole existed. By being either there or not, the holes acted with exactly the kind of binary precision that appealed to Charles Babbage (see page 16), who even ordered a portrait of Jacquard to be woven on one of his looms, which required 24,000 punch cards.

RELATED TOPICS
See also
THE DIFFERENCE ENGINE
page 16

MECHANICAL COMPUTERS
page 24

3-SECOND BIOGRAPHIES
JAMES WATT
1736–1819
Scottish inventor who made the steam engine practical in 1765, effectively launching the first Industrial Revolution

JOSEPH-MARIE JACQUARD
1752–1834
French weaver and merchant awarded the Legion of Honour for inventing the automated loom

30-SECOND TEXT
Adam Juniper

Joseph-Marie Jacquard invented the automated loom, growing the textile industry in France.

THE DIFFERENCE ENGINE

the 30-second code

3-SECOND BIT
If built, this would have been the world's first mechanical computer, using 25,000 parts and weighing 14 tonnes, to calculate up to 5th-order polynomials (equations with multiple numbers).

3-MINUTE BYTE
Babbage's machines used decimal numbers, not binary, which significantly added to the mechanical complexity. Computer scientist Konrad Zuse realized this and in 1937 built his first computer, the 1000kg Z1, in his parents' basement. Although motor driven, the computer had memory and floating-point logic and was freely programmable (by holes punched in 35mm film).

Charles Babbage's Difference Engine is often seen as the first mechanical computer. Babbage is credited with a variety of inventions but the mathematics tables of the day moved him to embark upon his most famous experiment: a mechanical computer. In 1822, after three years of experimentation, he impressed the British government enough to grant him £1,700 (over £200,000 today) to continue the work. The cost of manufacturing gears of the necessary quality proved challenging and the government eventually withdrew funding in 1842 (by which time £17,000 had been spent). That was not the end of Babbage's ambition though; he also envisaged a machine called the Analytical Engine, which was a real computer that could be programmed using punch cards. If ever built, it would have been bigger than a railway locomotive, with the 'mill' (processor) taking up one end, with a 'store' (memory) at the other end. Designing the Analytical Engine also inspired the second Difference Engine, however, the former was never built and the latter was not constructed until 1991 (when the London Science Museum secured the funding). In the decades that followed Babbage's work, mechanical means would be refined, if not in computing, then in related tasks, not least the 1890 census in the US.

RELATED TOPICS
See also
THE INDUSTRIAL REVOLUTION
page 14

HUMAN COMPUTERS
page 20

3-SECOND BIOGRAPHIES
CHARLES BABBAGE
1791–1871
English polymath known in many fields, from mechanics, economics and astronomy to investigating ghosts

KONRAD ZUSE
1910–95
Created the Z3, the first Turing-complete computer, in 1941, in Berlin. Unnoticed by the West until 1946

30-SECOND TEXT
Adam Juniper

Charles Babbage was known for his experimental designs, including the Difference Engine.

10 December 1815
Born in London, England

1816
Lord Byron signs the 'deed of separation' with Ada's mother and leaves

1829
A bout of measles leaves her paralysed for over a year

1833
Babbage invites Lovelace to see his prototype Difference Engine

1835
Marries Baron William King, giving her access to three homes (one in Surrey, one in London and one in Scotland).

1838
Queen Victoria makes William King an earl, making Ada the Countess of Lovelace

1840
Lovelace renews communication with Babbage, discussing the calculus she was studying

1842–3
Translates Luigi Menabrea's article on Babbage's machine, adding her famous notes

Sep 1843
Babbage (not seen as reliable with government money) agrees to work on the Analytical Engine and allows Lovelace to promote it

1844
Tells her friend Woronzow Greig she wants to create a mathematical model of the brain

1851
In May the Great Exhibition in Crystal Palace is the high point of Victorian Technology; Ada and Babbage's circle are all involved

1852
She confesses something to her husband from her deathbed, and he abandons her

27 November 1852
Dies, aged 36, from uterine cancer (not helped by the bloodletting treatment of the day).

2002
The Science Museum, London, finally builds the Difference Engine from plans

ADA LOVELACE

The only legitimate daughter of poet Lord Byron (as close as the age came to a rock star), Augusta Ada King, Countess of Lovelace had limited knowledge of her father, who separated from her mother a month after her birth, left England soon after and died of disease in Greece when Ada was eight. Ada and her mother were not close, some historians say her mother's bitterness towards her ex-husband persuaded her to steer Ada away from any artistic tendencies by pushing her towards mathematics and logic. Ada encountered numerous celebrated figures, including Charles Dickens and Michael Faraday. Most significantly, in 1833, when she was 18, she met and began working with scientist Charles Babbage, known by many as the 'father of the computer'.

When they met, Babbage was refining his Difference Engine, a mechanical calculator, and as he worked on that, the Analytical Engine occurred to him too – in essence the first modern computer (see page 16). As his assistant, Lovelace became fascinated by the prototype mechanical computers. Her ability to understand the temperamental Babbage helped him get his ideas to the academic community (and learn from it). Famously, in 1842–3, when Lovelace translated an Italian article about Babbage's proposed machine, she added extensive notes (tripling its length), not least because the British academic establishment didn't immediately see the possibilities of the proposed engine. One of Ada's notes (Note G) was an example program (to calculate Bernoulli numbers) and, in effect, the first-ever computer algorithm, in which Lovelace invented the computer loop.

Babbage was appreciative, calling her 'the Enchantress of Number' when writing to thank her. Aside from a brief squabble over Babbage's desire to criticize the government (for not funding his machines), the two remained friends. So much so that he was a regular visitor to Lovelace's marital home, Worthy Manor, Somerset, and the spot they paced and theorized has since been renamed 'Philosopher's Walk'. Babbage was not the only one to be enchanted by Lovelace; she had an affair with a tutor in 1833, and was rumoured to have many affairs in the 1840s, as well as apparently setting up a gambling syndicate with male friends that lost her £3,000 (the world was yet to be excited by computers).

Adam Juniper

HUMAN COMPUTERS

the 30-second code

3-SECOND BIT
Before the word 'computer' applied to devices, it referred to someone with the job of performing calculations.

3-MINUTE BYTE
In 1948, calculating the path of a rocket at JPL took all day and there were so many female computers that some engineers were dismissing it as 'women's work'. As a result, the new IBM computers of the 1950s were often handed on to the women, who in turn took on many programming roles despite the era's conventions.

Deep in the 21st century, the term 'computer' has a pretty established meaning, but the act of solving, or computing, a mathematical equation predates even Charles Babbage's mechanical calculators. The word 'computer' didn't appear in the dictionary in the sense we now know it until 1946. As far back as the 1600s, writer Sir Thomas Browne used it to refer to individuals recalculating dates in the conversion from Julian to Gregorian calendars. Before digital computers, large teams existed to perform calculations. One of the most famous was California's Jet Propulsion Laboratory (JPL), which was set up by a few California Institute of Technology (Caltech) students (and rocket enthusiasts) in the mid-1930s, but eventually became a key part of NASA. During the Second World War the JPL team worked on day-to-day calculations such as how many extra booster rockets would be needed to help lift Japan-bound bombers into the air. As the Apollo space program developed, more calculations were needed and Barbara 'Barby' Canright, the first female computer, was joined by others. Some, such as Helen Ling, became supervisors and – in a time before maternity leave – are credited with promising to re-hire female computers after pregnancy. Despite their significant achievements, the computers worked in rooms adjoining the more famous Mission Control.

RELATED TOPICS
See also
THE INDUSTRIAL REVOLUTION
page 14

CODEBREAKERS
page 26

3-SECOND BIOGRAPHIES
KATHERINE JOHNSON
1918–2020
African-American teacher-turned-computer who worked for NASA for over three decades, earning the Medal of Freedom (inspiring the film *Hidden Figures*)

BARBARA CANRIGHT
1919–97
American mathematician, the first female computer at the Jet Propulsion Laboratory (JPL), working from 1939

30-SECOND TEXT
Adam Juniper

Barbara Canright was NASA's first female 'human computer', calculating by hand with pencil and graph paper.

TASK-SPECIFIC COMPUTERS

the 30-second code

3-SECOND BIT
Before programmable computers existed, machines built specifically to handle large data projects, such as censuses, developed reliable technology for storing information.

3-MINUTE BYTE
Having established a monopoly on information storage, punch cards were inevitably adopted by early computers. IBM's first general-purpose computer, the IBM 701, accepted cards in a fixed format, in which each of the now-standard 80 lines indicated either an address, an operation or a note. By the 1960s, computer languages such as Fortran could be programmed via these cards.

Since Jacquard's loom showed that devices could, in effect, store data (on holes punched in card), many inventors used what we now recognize as computing principles to automate elements of their designs. In 1890, Herman Hollerith succeeded in getting his punch card tabulating machine adopted in the New York State Census and from there secured contracts with the US government for the 1900 census and New York railroads. Hollerith's innovation was not cards – indeed he failed to get that patent because Babbage's Analytical Engine (see page 16) already used them. He did, however, much improve upon the mechanism for reading information from cards, and set the standard size of 186 x 83mm (7⅜ x 3¼ in) for future punch cards (which, before 1929, were the size of US banknotes). These machines for reading information from cards, known as tabulators, were less complicated than the Analytical Engine. In a typical retail use, a deck of cards, each punched with price fields and accompanying categories, would be inserted into a tabulator. It would sum all the prices in each category. Hollerith formed a company to supply his format of cards and tabulators and called it Hollerith's Tabulating Machine Corporation. Financier Charles Flint later merged it with other ventures exploring the technology and called his new monolith IBM.

RELATED TOPICS
See also
THE INDUSTRIAL REVOLUTION
page 14

THE DIFFERENCE ENGINE
page 16

3-SECOND BIOGRAPHY
HERMAN HOLLERITH
1860–1929
American businessman, inventor and statistician; his 'Hollerith Machine' for automated tabulating of punch cards launched IBM

30-SECOND TEXT
Adam Juniper

Herman Hollerith's tabulating machine read cards by passing them through electrical contacts.

MECHANICAL COMPUTERS

the 30-second code

The idea of holding and processing information in a binary, on/off manner is seen as the only way computers can work these days. This was not always the case, though; while modern components need to work with a single voltage and electronic switches, those who first imagined computing devices had no such heritage to build on. Their experience of machines was more mechanical. Charles Babbage's early designs were constructed from wheels that turned in any of ten different directions (representing each digit). That's a lot more than the two positions – 0 and 1 – associated with binary. In the years that followed Babbage, machines were built using ball-and-disc integrators. These integrators were composed of a spinning disc turning at a fixed rate and a cylinder connected to a mechanical wheel with output numbers. Between the two was a bearing, which transferred the motion from the disc to the cylinder. If the bearing was near the middle, the cylinder would turn very slowly, but positioned nearer the faster-moving rim, it would turn the cylinder more quickly. Machines set to expected positions of the Moon were used by the Royal Navy to calculate tides and gunnery ranges. The Navy's Dreadnought-class vessels were so powerful that human spotters weren't able to accurately determine range alone so, by 1914, up to 50 crew might operate integrators.

RELATED TOPICS
See also
THE DIFFERENCE ENGINE
page 16

HUMAN COMPUTERS
page 20

3-SECOND BIOGRAPHIES
LORD KELVIN
(WILLIAM THOMSON)
1824–1907
Mathematical physicist known for formulating the first and second rules of thermodynamics; knighted for his work on the transatlantic telegraph and for whom the Kelvin scale is named

FREDERIC CHARLES DREYER
1878–1956
Royal Navy officer and admiral who fought in the battle of Jutland and designed a mechanical computer (The Dreyer Table) to calculate gunnery range, which was chosen above the Navy's preferred contractor

30-SECOND TEXT
Adam Juniper

Machines built using ball-and-disc integrators were used by the Royal Navy and in German V2 rocket bombs.

3-SECOND BIT
Early calculating devices assisted in calculations by translating numbers into analogue measurements.

3-MINUTE BYTE
Following the Royal Navy's innovation, many calculating tools using this principle were created, including the US Navy's rangekeeper, torpedo data calculators and the famous Norden bombsight. On the other side, similar principles were used by the mechanical controls placed behind the warhead in the German V2 rocket bombs.

COMBUSTION CHAMBER
AND VENTURI

TURBINE AND
PUMP ASSEMBLY

ALCOHOL TANK

LIQUID OXYGEN TANK

CONTROL COMPARTMENT

EXTERNAL CONTROL VANES

INTERNAL
CONTROL VANES

OCTOBER · NOVEMBER · DECEMBER · JANUARY · FEBRUARY

A. Lege & C.º

LONDON

JULY · JUNE · MAY

5 6

6 5 4 3 2

CODEBREAKERS

the 30-second code

In 1938, when the British government realized the inevitability of conflict with Germany, it moved the Government Code and Cypher School to Bletchley Park. The decrypted messages, sent in the German Enigma code, were called 'Ultra' intelligence, and are credited with taking years off the war and saving 14 million lives. The Enigma encryption was created using mechanical devices based around wheels that moved position after each new character was added to the message. New settings were fed into these machines each day, so speed in working out the encryption settings, which could then be used for the decrypts, was essential. This presented the team – especially Alan Turing and Gordon Welchman – with the incentive to develop electromechanical solutions. The first of these, Bombe, was built largely from tabulating machine components. Later, another code, Lorenz, led to the construction of Colossus, which was programmable and replaced an unreliable paper feed with thermionic valves (or 'tubes'). Classified as top secret, it took 50 years for the British government to acknowledge the achievements at Bletchley, and it is known that a Colossus decrypt revealed to US General Dwight Eisenhower that Hitler believed the D-Day preparations were merely a bluff, which persuaded the general to proceed with the Normandy landings.

RELATED TOPICS
See also
MECHANICAL COMPUTERS
page 24

ALAN TURING
page 150

3-SECOND BIT
The first semi-programmable electronic computer, Colossus, was built to help crack German codes during the Second World War.

3-MINUTE BYTE
The German Enigma code had billions of combinations and should have been virtually unbreakable, but insights from Polish spies and a lack of German discipline – including adding the same words, 'Heil Hitler', at the end of virtually all communications – gave Bletchley the openings it needed.

3-SECOND BIOGRAPHIES
MAX NEWMAN
1897–1984
British mathematician and codebreaker who, after the war, developed the world's first stored-program electronic computer, the Manchester Baby, in 1948

TOMMY FLOWERS
1905–98
British engineer who worked with the telecommunications division of the Post Office and built Colossus

30-SECOND TEXT
Adam Juniper

The activities at Bletchley Park crucially broke the German Enigma code during The Second World War.

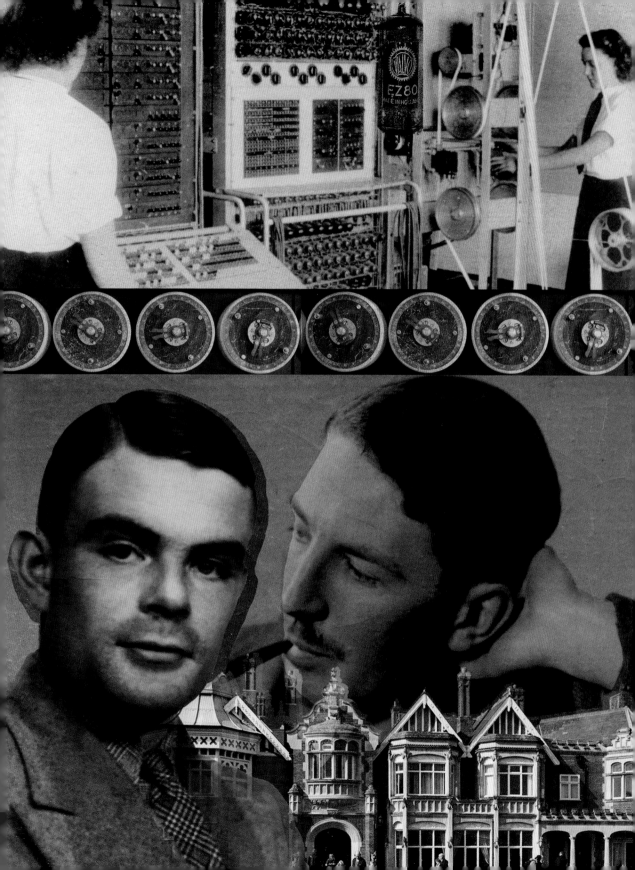

INSTRUCTION SETS & STORED PROGRAMS

the 30-second code

3-SECOND BIT
The basis of computer science is describing tasks in terms of programs, a concept first invented before computers even existed.

3-MINUTE BYTE
From Turing's theoretical instruction book, the computer's 'instruction set' emerged. This is a list of the most fundamental instructions that can be sent to the processor – commands such as ADD (to add two numbers together) or JUMP to jump to a designated memory address. The term 'instruction set' can refer to all the instructions for a particular processor, or a certain subset.

Bletchley Park didn't come from nowhere. Alan Turing had, in 1936, written a paper, 'On Computable Numbers', addressing the problems of building reprogrammable calculating devices. Existing methods, such as plugboards with moveable cables, seemed inadequate and Turing proposed a 'Universal Computing Machine' that could tackle anything that any other task-specific machine (or human computer) could do. Turing's observations of others performing calculations was that, at the most fundamental level, they read a number, performed an action based on that number, then moved on to another place. He posited that a (potentially lengthy) book of instructions could be created to describe every possible task in the format 'if you read x, print y, then read the digit z' – in other words, the book of instructions was a computer program and every single action was like a conditional statement. Turing's paper hammered home that the technology of the day made each of the steps possible, as the machine needs only be 'aware' of a single symbol, perform one action, then go to whichever page in the instructions it's told to next. The University of Manchester's 'Baby' ran its first program in 1948. It marked the first time that electronic components were used for the memory that held the program, as opposed to plugboard wires or cards, which could take a long time to reprogram.

RELATED TOPICS
See also
ADA LOVELACE
page 18

CODEBREAKERS
page 26

ALAN TURING
page 150

3-SECOND BIOGRAPHY
DAVID HILBERT
1862–1943
German mathematician credited with challenging the academic community to develop a practical method of taking on the task of thinking; for example, answering 'yes' or 'no' as to the truth of a mathematical statement

30-SECOND TEXT
Adam Juniper

The University of Manchester's 'Baby' incorporated Alan Turing's mathematical concepts.

BUF-IEC	INV-IEC	AND-IEC	NAND-IEC	OR-IEC	NOR-IEC	XOR-IEC	XNOR-IEC

BUF-US	INV-US	AND-US	NAND-US	OR-US	NOR-US	XOR-US	XNOR-US

BUF-DE	INV-DE	AND-DE	NAND-DE	OR-DE	NOR-DE	XOR-DE	XNOR-DE

THE FETCH-EXECUTE CYCLE
the 30-second code

The fetch-execute cycle is the process a computer uses to achieve the most basic element of a calculation, like an individual line from Turing's instruction book. Programming, in essence, is ordering the correct fetch-execute cycles in sequence. Fetch-execute is a fancy way of saying 'get and do', and you've certainly encountered the term 'executable' (or '.exe') before on a computer. So, wrapping that all up, an executable file is the instruction book Turing described. Breaking it down a little further, some might say that the process is more correctly known as 'fetch-decode-execute', because it starts with the address (in the computer's memory) of the next instruction. Getting that and copying it to the current instruction register (CIR) is the first part of the fetch-execute cycle. Only after this is the value of the program counter – the internal clock – advanced by one and the instruction carried out. This will involve sending signals from the processor to the memory or other components via the control bus. This process goes on all the time in a processor core, and it is this that is measured by the clock speed. The faster the computer, the more cycles. It is also why turning the power off effectively resets the machine; each of these pulses is electricity. Remove it and you remove the system's blood, including that which flows to the immediate memory.

RELATED TOPICS
See also
ASSEMBLY LANGUAGE
page 40

COMPILED CODE
page 48

3-SECOND BIOGRAPHY
JOHN VON NEUMANN
1903–57
A Hungarian-American polymath who proposed the fetch-execute cycle. He also pre-empted the discovery of DNA and worked on the Manhattan Project

30-SECOND TEXT
Adam Juniper

3-SECOND BIT
The central processing unit (CPU) of a computer handles instructions one after another until there are none left.

3-MINUTE BYTE
One line of modern programming isn't the same as one fetch-execute cycle. Just to add some numbers, a computer will need code to load the numbers, to store them as variables in its active memory registers (which means an operation for each number), to do the adding, then to store the result. It'll likely also need to send the result to another variable.

Ordering the correct fetch-execute cycles in sequence is the essence of programming.

THE TRANSISTOR REVOLUTION

the 30-second code

Mechanical calculators had cogs, gears and many possible positions, or 'states', for each number. Modern computers, however, represent these states with voltages. More states on each cog made for fiddly engineering, but it reduced the overall number of cogs, resulting in a simpler device. The next step, eliminating mechanics altogether, meant using voltages to represent numbers. Having any more than two possible states (on and off) would require computers to be filled with devices that could measure voltages. Since these devices were not small or reliable, the more practical solution was to use what is called Boolean logic: to say a voltage is 'on' and the lack of voltage is 'off' and have these represent 1 (True) or 0 (False). With just two possibilities, all computer operations can be reduced down to very simple circuits with two inputs and one output. These are called logic gates, and there are basically just three types: conjunction (AND), disjunction (OR) and negation (NOT). In early computers, such as the ENIAC, these tasks were performed by vacuum tubes called triodes, but it was rare for a machine to last a whole day without one of its 18,000 triodes failing. Finding a more robust technology was essential to radio, communications and early computing, and in 1947 a team at Bell Laboratories pulled it off, creating the transistor.

RELATED TOPICS

See also
THE DIFFERENCE ENGINE
page 16

ADA LOVELACE
page 18

CODEBREAKERS
page 26

THE PERSONAL
COMPUTER AGE
page 34

3-SECOND BIT

Transistors replaced the unreliable lightbulb-sized tubes that made radios and early computers impractical.

3-MINUTE BYTE

Transistors were made using a 'semiconductive' material and 'semiconductor' is another term you'll hear used to describe them (and microprocessors with many, many transistors). It took time for transistors to shrink (the famous Sony TR-63 'pocket' radio came in 1957), but size was less of an issue when the University of Manchester completed the world's first transistor computer in November 1953.

3-SECOND BIOGRAPHY
RICHARD GRIMSDALE
1929–2005
Born in Australia, Grimsdale moved to England to go to Manchester University (he was a student while Alan Turing was there) and went on to build the first transistorized computer, the Metrovick 950, in 1953

30-SECOND TEXT
Adam Juniper

Transistors revolutionized portable consumer electronics.

THE PERSONAL COMPUTER AGE

the 30-second code

3-SECOND BIT
With all the technology in place, the final step was for all but a few computing brands to be eliminated, creating a big enough market for useful software applications to be worth creating, and to take on previously manual tasks.

3-MINUTE BYTE
Acorn's enthusiasm for creating its own silicon has meant that one aspect of their technology has outlasted the company itself (unlike so many other computer companies from that generation). Its creation, the ARM chip, outlived Acorn's range of PCs and was spun off. It is now used, under license, by all phone processor manufacturers and forms the basis of Apple's own computer processors (introduced in 2020).

With transistors discovered and refined into microchips (onto which millions of transistors are drawn into single components), the ingredients were in place for cheap, mass-produced computers. Only one issue remained, but it was a big one: compatibility. During the 1980s, your choice of computer had a dramatic effect on which software you could use. A great example is a small British company, Acorn. Between 1979 and 1997 Acorn created a range of several computer systems with varying components, some they designed themselves. The company targeted specific markets with tailored machines (hobby, commercial, education and home), offered several generations of processor, and each machine used different sizes of disk or cassette to store materials. Despite all that innovation, Acorn was just one player that barely got out of its home market, and far from the only one. In 1984 demand for home computers had peaked, but offerings from Atari, Commodore, Apple and other big names flooded the market to the point that no one sold enough to create a sustainable software market. At the same time, the business world was standardizing on DOS (typed commands) and eventually Microsoft Windows. While there were questionable marketing practices, the result was an established, dominant computing platform at an accessible price.

RELATED TOPICS
See also
INSTRUCTION SETS & STORED PROGRAMS
page 28

THE TRANSISTOR REVOLUTION
page 32

3-SECOND BIOGRAPHIES
CHRIS CURRY
1946–
British technology inventor and entrepreneur who worked with Clive Sinclair before leaving to set up Acorn Computers to compete for the BBC Micro contract

SOPHIE WILSON
1957–
British computer scientist and Cambridge graduate who joined Acorn Computers, noted for assembling the prototype BBC Micro and designing the ARM instruction set

30-SECOND TEXT
Adam Juniper

The refinement of transistors into microchips kick-started the personal computer revolution.

INSTRUCTING COMPUTERS

INSTRUCTING COMPUTERS
GLOSSARY

abstraction Looking at a situation and eliminating any elements – physical or temporal – in order to create code that does what is needed and no more. As opposed to an abstract type in the code of a program, which allows you to create methods that are not used.

application (app) The common term for a computer program designed to be used to perform a function (for example, word processor) as opposed to software designed to run the computer.

C One of the first programming languages, this is foundational for Python among others. As it is older, it is more useful for programming hardware than web apps. The more modern extension, C++, does have uses in computer games and simulations.

C# Pronounced 'see sharp', this is a variant of the language C with Microsoft's .NET framework built in.

cloud General term for internet-based (remote) storage or application services.

executable file As opposed to the code for a program, an executable file is the application that can be run on a computer. For Windows users they are .exe files.

GitHub A web-based hosting service for sharing code. Originally built on a code management system (called Git) by Linus Torvalds, it was acquired by Microsoft.

Go Developed by Google (as Golang) as a readable and secure language able to process data, but is not widely popular.

'goto' statement An instruction in code to jump to another point in the program.

hexadecimal Or 'hex' for short. A system of counting using base 16 that is frequently used in computing (and colour picking in web design). This uses the digits 0123456789ABCDEF so, for example, the number 12 would be represented as 'C', while 16 would be '10'.

Java The programming language associated with client-server applications thanks to its 'write-once, run anywhere' design.

low-level language Provides little, if any, change to the programming concepts of the computer itself, for example, assembly language and machine code.

machine code The lowest level of computer program that can be fed into a system to make it run. It is difficult to write (typically in binary) and not portable to other systems, but allows some programmers to ensure the fastest possible operation. Assembly language is slightly easier (some human-readable commands), but structurally similar.

open source A project in which the developers make the source code available to others (though not necessarily for free; openness is more about facilitating compatibility).

Python A high-level, object-orientated interpreted programming language first released in 1991. Python is designed to make code easy to read with space around the characters. Has integrations with C and C++.

Ruby A language that provided a framework for web applications and is still used for some, though Python, PHP, Node JS and JavaScript have all overtaken it.

server A computer that provides data to any others (either on a local network or the internet). Common examples are web servers (web pages), mail servers (email) and file servers (large-scale, usually backed-up file storage).

Smalltalk An object-orientated programming language developed alongside Windows-based computing at Xerox PARC.

source code In a compiled language, this is the relatively easy-to-read language that the program is written in.

stack register If your code is being run, in order, from the computer's memory, it must also be stored in that memory. The stack register keeps it in order, like line numbers, so it can be found.

variable In programming, all data being manipulated needs to be stored in the computer's memory. A space is allocated for each piece of data and given a name so the program can access it – this is the variable.

Xerox PARC A research facility of the office equipment company where Alan Kay and others famously developed the graphical user interface (GUI). Their work 'inspired' Steve Jobs, among others, who once said 'Xerox could have owned the entire computer industry'.

ASSEMBLY LANGUAGE

the 30-second code

3-SECOND BIT
With its focus on efficiency and performance, assembly language is used in embedded smart devices (such as smart thermostats) and fast-moving video games.

3-MINUTE BYTE
Assembly language and machine code are low-level programming languages. The way they're written makes them hard for humans to understand. Contrast this with high-level programming languages, such as Python and Ruby, which use English words. High-level languages abstract away low-level concepts, such as memory management, and deal with the complexities of running the same code on different processors. Low-level languages produce hardware-specific code, which can get the best performance from the processor.

Code tells a computer what to do.

However, humans don't speak the same language as computers. A computer's central processing unit (CPU) takes instructions in binary, or machine code: 0s and 1s. Machine code is not portable between different processor families: each type of CPU (for example, Intel or ARM) has its own specific hardware and architecture and only understands the corresponding machine code. It is also difficult for humans to work directly with machine code. Assembly language bridges the gap, allowing us to write a set of more readable commands that closely mirror the instructions the processor natively understands. We write assembly language as a series of statements, using mnemonics. Each statement is made up of an opcode and an operand. The opcode gives the processor a single action to carry out, for example, define a variable. The operand, often written in hexadecimal, tells the processor where the data is stored, or gives it the data that needs to be stored to execute the instruction. The computer can translate the assembly code directly into machine code using a software package called an assembler. Once the assembler translates the assembly code into machine code, the computer can run it again and again without needing to reassemble it.

RELATED TOPICS
See also
COMPILED CODE
page 48

OBJECT-ORIENTED
PROGRAMMING (OOP)
page 50

3-SECOND BIOGRAPHY
SIR MAURICE
VINCENT WILKES
1913–2010
British computer scientist and Turing Award winner who created microcode: an organization layer between CPU and programmer, which led to assembly language

30-SECOND TEXT
Suze Shardlow

Assembly language bridges the gap between human language and machine code.

```
                    * CALLS: none
                    * DESCRIPTION: Gets 1 character from terminal

)10 B6 80 04   INCH       LDA A   ACIA        GET STATUS
)13 47                    ASR A               SHIFT RDRF FLAG INTO CARRY
)14 24 FA                 BCC     INCH        RECIEVE NOT READY
)16 B6 80 05              LDA A   ACIA+1      GET CHAR
)19 84 7F                 AND A   #$7F        MASK PARITY
)1B 7E C0 79              JMP     OUTCH       ECHO & RTS


               *******************************************
               * FUNCTION: INHEX - INPUT HEX DIGIT
               * INPUT: none
```

FORTRAN: THE FIRST HIGH-LEVEL LANGUAGE

the 30-second code

3-SECOND BIT
High-level languages abstract user commands from the electromechanical switching inside the components.

3-MINUTE BYTE
The creation of so-called 'high-level' languages effectively introduced the concept of translators, or compilers, into the computing process. Compiled code now forms part of the artificial wall between the 'user' and the 'developer', and modern systems do not necessarily make it straightforward to access the original code (source code) behind a program.

Developed by IBM in the 1950s, Fortran, a short form of 'Formula Translation', remains a general-purpose programming language. In 1957 it was the result of a project initiated by John W. Backus at IBM, who had realized that creating computer programs in assembly language resulted in an impractical level of debugging and wouldn't help sell computers. While giving the computer an assembler prevented some of the tiresome programming mechanics of keeping track of memory addresses, Dr Grace Hopper, working on the Harvard Mark I computer had already created Arithmetic Language Mark Zero (A-0) – the first computer language with a compiler – in 1952. In an assembly language, there was a direct one-to-one mapping of command to instruction in the processor, so at best it would be slightly more linguistically friendly. A-0 was the first language not to do that, with some brief commands requiring the processor to perform several cycles. This, in turn, necessitated a compiler – to translate A-0 to assembly language – and Hopper also created the first of these. Not that her peers were suitably impressed, 'I had a working compiler, and nobody would touch it,' said Hopper. Only a year later, Backus's project at IBM resulted in Fortran, a language that was often represented on punch cards (one statement per card).

RELATED TOPICS
See also
ASSEMBLY LANGUAGE
page 40

GRACE HOPPER
page 44

3-SECOND BIOGRAPHY
JOHN W. BACKUS
1924–2007
Created high-level programming languages Speedcoding and Fortran, the first to gain wide-level use; Won the Turing Award

30-SECOND TEXT
Adam Juniper

Dr Grace Hopper created A-0, the first computer language with a compiler.

9 December 1906
Born in New York City, USA

1934
Achieves PhD in maths from Yale – one of only 1,279 in the last 72 years

1940
Attempts to enlist in the US Navy during the Second World War but is rejected as, at 34, she is too old

1941
Promoted to associate professor after a decade teaching at Vassar College

1944
Joins the Harvard Mark I computer programming staff

1947
Discovers a moth stuck in a computer relay, solving an issue – sometimes credited as coining the terms 'bug' and 'debug' (within the field of computing, at least) and the bug's remains are held in the Smithsonian

1949
Joins the Eckert-Mauchly team that developed UNIVAC 1 computer

1952
Completes her 'linker' or 'compiler'

1954
Eckert-Mauchly chooses Hopper to lead a department for automatic programming

1959
CODASYL conference launches COBOL, the new business language

1967
The US Navy recalls her to active duty a year after she retires from the Naval Reserve

1986
Retirement ceremony on US Navy's oldest commissioned ship, the USS *Constitution*

1 January 1992
Dies in her sleep, aged 85

GRACE HOPPER

Grace Brewster Murray Hopper was born in New York to Scottish and Dutch parents. She became a computer scientist and one of the first programmers on the Harvard Mark I computer, and a Rear Admiral in the United States Navy. This level of achievement wasn't lost on her peers, who nicknamed her 'Amazing Grace', although at a younger age her expertise was more commonly demonstrated by dismantling devices such as alarm clocks.

A graduate of Vassar with a master's degree from Yale, she was rejected by the US Navy when she tried to enlist during the Second World War because she was, at 34, too old and fell below the minimum weight requirement. However, she was allowed to become top of her class in the Naval Reserve and in 1944 joined the Bureau of Ships Computation Project at Harvard, which led her to the Mark I computer programming staff led by Howard H. Aiken, with whom she went on to co-author three papers. After the war she stayed at Harvard under her Navy contract rather than going back to Vassar as a professor.

She was lured away from academia by the Eckert-Mauchly Computer Corporation in 1949 to develop the UNIVAC, the first large-scale electronic computer on the market. There she was warned off her new programming language idea 'because computers didn't understand English'. She persevered, writing a paper on the subject of linkers, or compilers, and eventually her ideas – the compiler known as the A compiler and the language A-0 – made it through. Subsequently, she began work on refining it into a language, which, in 1959, was called the Common Business-Orientated Language (COBOL) and went on to become one of the most ubiquitous computer-programming languages of the late 20th century.

Hopper retired from the Navy several times, first at the age of 60 (in accordance with regulations) with the rank of Commander. She was recalled for a six-month assignment, which was extended indefinitely, retiring again in 1971, but was asked to return to active duty in 1972, finally retiring in 1986 as Commodore (and the oldest active-duty commissioned officer).

Adam Juniper

PROCEDURAL LANGUAGES

the 30-second code

The grammar of computing

languages evolved with their development, beginning with the strictest low-level operations, described in machine code. The first advance was assembly language, which enabled some code reuse and logical functions (instructions such as READ and GET). This is a second-generation language. The third generation (which was first called 'high-level language') is known as procedural, because it operates in steps, one after the other, like a procedure. Different languages offered different vocabulary, typically designed to be easier for experts in the field to understand; famous examples are COBOL, FORTRAN, BASIC and C (though not C++, an object-based language). To ensure that a procedure can take place in order, and to ensure the additional benefit of being able to move to a different point in a program, the procedures need to be sequenced. That means line numbers, or an equivalent, can be translated to memory addresses when the program is moved to RAM (random access memory) before being executed by the processor. That, in turn, means an area of the memory is designated as the 'stack register'. Another way to look at it is, if a procedural program in memory is viewed like a table, the first column of that table is the stack register.

RELATED TOPICS
See also
ASSEMBLY LANGUAGE
page 40

FORTRAN: THE FIRST
HIGH-LEVEL LANGUAGE
page 42

3-SECOND BIOGRAPHIES
JOHN G. KEMENY
1926–92
Hungarian-born American, Einstein's mathematical assistant at graduate school, and 13th president of Dartmouth College who co-created BASIC

THOMAS E. KURTZ
1928–
Co-creator of BASIC and director of the ground-breaking multidisciplinary Information Systems programme at Dartmouth College

30-SECOND TEXT
Adam Juniper

3-SECOND BIT
A procedural language is one in which all the instructions exist in sequence like a stack.

3-MINUTE BYTE
If modern programmers call your code 'procedural', they're not usually being complimentary – the term is associated with early computing and programs littered with 'goto' statements that programmers considered damaging to the code's structure. In reality, procedural languages can be very useful, but object-oriented (OO) languages such as Ruby dominate the coding landscape.

Procedural language operates in steps, one after another, to resemble a stack.

COMMODORE BASIC
7167 BYTES FREE
READY.
709
MOVE LW-PARM-VAL TO WW-NUM-ELEMS
PERFORM B001-NEW-ARRAY
COMPUTE WW-INCREMENT =
WW-NUM-ELEMS / 200000
END-COMPUTE
PERFORM VARYING WW-ARRAY-IDX FROM 1 BY WW-INCREMENT
UNTIL WW-ARRAY-IDX > WW-NUM-ELEMS
MOVE WW-ARRAY-IDX TO WW-DATA
03 LW-PARM-LEN
03 LW-PARM-VAL
PROCEDURE DIVISION USING LW-PARM.
A001-MAINLINE SECTION.
PERFORM B001-NEW-ARRAY
professional computer
2001 Series

COMPILED CODE

the 30-second code

A computer processor cannot understand a high-level language such as C or Go. It can only understand machine code. Many coding jobs (for example in web or mobile app development), however, involve high-level languages. Programmers write what's called source code, which then needs to be converted into machine code so the processor can run it. One way of doing this is by using a compiler. The compiler turns source code into machine code to prepare it for execution. Successful compilation results in an executable file, which the processor can then run directly. Certain classes of error can be detected by the compilation process, including missing punctuation. We must fix these before the compiler will output an executable. This process improves overall reliability by identifying and eliminating such errors before the code is allowed to run. In this regard, it's like baking a cake. We don't usually consume the raw ingredients individually. We mix them according to our recipe, then put the mixture in the oven. Then we wait to see if our method has worked. If the cake comes out well, we can eat it. If not, we need to re-measure and re-mix the ingredients and re-bake the cake.

3-SECOND BIT
A compiler transforms code written in a high-level programming language into a machine code executable file, which a processor can understand and run directly.

3-MINUTE BYTE
The advantages of compiled code come with disadvantages. Compiled programs run faster because compilation converts them to processor-specific machine code. However, the code-run-debug cycle can be slower for the computer programmer as compilation takes time and needs to be performed every time a change is made to the source code, no matter how small.

RELATED TOPICS
See also
ASSEMBLY LANGUAGE
page 40

FORTRAN: THE FIRST
HIGH-LEVEL LANGUAGE
page 42

MAKING CODE PORTABLE
page 78

3-SECOND BIOGRAPHIES
DENNIS RITCHIE
1941–2011
Turing Award winner (with Ken Thompson) and creator of the C programming language; played a key part in developing UNIX

KEN THOMPSON
1943–
A pioneer of computer science, working at Bell Laboratories where he created B (predecessor of C), helped develop UNIX and went on to be co-creator of Go at Google

30-SECOND TEXT
Suze Shardlow

The compiler turns source code into machine code, which a processer can understand and run directly.

OBJECT-ORIENTED PROGRAMMING (OOP)

the 30-second code

Code often takes in data, processes it and gives us an output. Object-oriented programming (OOP) is a programming structure where data and its related code sit together in an object. This arrangement offers advantages, including reusability, readability, better performance and easier debugging and maintenance. For our objects, we define a class, attributes and methods. The class is a template, for example, passenger aircraft. The class says each object has attributes, in this case model, wings, seats, engines and fuel capacity. Finally, the methods are the code that manipulates each object, such as calculating fuel consumption. We can use inheritance, one of the four principles of OOP, to create 'child' objects (Boeing 747-400ER, 747-400ERF, 747-400F) from a 'parent' object (747-400) to reduce duplication. Properties or code are duplicated unless otherwise stated. Polymorphism, another of the tenets, allows us to define specific methods for each child, such as for calculating flight range and centre of gravity. Encapsulation protects an object's attributes from being modified from outside (the number of engines on a plane remains fixed) and the final principle, abstraction, means a method can run without knowing the fine details of the other methods: we can calculate fuel consumption without details of how the fuel travels through the wings.

RELATED TOPICS
See also
PROCEDURAL LANGUAGES
page 46

CODE LIBRARIES
page 52

3-SECOND BIOGRAPHY
ALAN KAY
1940–
Turing Award winner and leader of the team at Xerox PARC that created the first OOP, Smalltalk and GUI. Apparently regrets coining the term 'objects' in this context as, in his words, 'the big idea is "messaging"'

30-SECOND TEXT
Suze Shardlow

3-SECOND BIT
Object-orientated languages have variables and procedures, like other languages, but offer more tools to re-use code and data, including classes, objects and inheritance.

3-MINUTE BYTE
OOP was created to facilitate writing large programs. As code became longer and more complex, any change could set off a chain reaction of bugs, which in turn were difficult to locate and fix. Abstraction and encapsulation allow programmers to focus on specific units of code and work more efficiently. Commonly-used object-oriented programming languages include C#, C++, Java, Python and Smalltalk.

Inheritance, one of the four principles of OOP, can be used to create 'child' objects from a 'parent' object.

CODE LIBRARIES

the 30-second code

3-SECOND BIT
In programming, a library is collection of reuseable functions. You can manage these in less or more sophisticated ways depending on the scale of your project.

3-MINUTE BYTE
Rather than include the source code, some code libraries operate using 'linkers'. Instead of inserting extra source code into your program before compiling into machine code, all the libraries are associated with pre-compiled machine code binaries. When your new program is compiled into a final binary, these sections are added in binary form, saving processing time.

At its core, a library is just a collection of written software functions that you can reuse at the beginning of a new program. You might choose to keep copies of functions you write in a long text file, then copy-and-paste at the start of new programs – this is a rudimentary library. This approach will get hard to manage over time, but programmers can keep pre-programmed tools ready in themed library files and link any they need. A computer's operating system might also include local libraries that can be accessed by software while it is being run, as discussed on the previous pages; the key is that the 'object' in the library works for any program that needs it. Programmers and entities such as businesses can share technologies (or at least the parts they wish to) via public code libraries, which is why open source is so often used to share features between programmers. Public code libraries create incredible potential, but the more entities involved, the greater the risk that updates of one tier of code could affect another, which is where the market for version tracking and management systems such as Microsoft's GitHub appeared.

RELATED TOPICS
See also
FUNCTIONS
page 76

AI: ARTIFICIAL INTELLIGENCE
page 138

30-SECOND TEXT
Adam Juniper

A code library is a collection of reusable functions that can be used at the beginning of a new program.

RUNNING CODE IN THE CLOUD

the 30-second code

3-SECOND BIT
Cloud computing is made of virtual computer servers so you can run programs as you need them.

3-MINUTE BYTE
Virtual Private Networks (VPNs) emerged in the 1990s as a way to balance the load and cost of computer servers (often marketed with clouds). In 2006 Amazon created a service that made this possible via a web interface, Amazon Web Services (AWS) or the 'Elastic Compute Cloud' – they moved Amazon.com onto this system in 2010.

For an online game (for example, email chess) we need a third computer connecting the players, which is responsible for setting up the board and emailing each player when it's their turn. That computer is a server, and the players' computers are clients. This is how the Web has worked for decades: we request a something (such as a web page) from a server, which grabs the page from network-attached storage and sends it. What would happen if one of our players went on holiday and didn't respond? Running a server idle for all that time wastes energy and money, but modern app design can help us out. Virtual machines are little slices of computing power that we can pay for and use when we want them. If we need a server for a weekend, we can request one from a pool of servers, do our work and then return it to the pool. This can even be handled automatically, so when the client sends their move, the server starts for the fraction of a second required to process the move, and bills the game's creator for that time only. The game can then be scaled to hundreds of thousands of people, without ever hitting capacity or wasting resources.

RELATED TOPICS
See also
OBJECT ORIENTED PROGRAMMING (OOP)
page 50

USER INTERFACE &EXPERIENCE
page 88

DATABASE OPERATION: CRUD
page 92

3-SECOND BIOGRAPHY
ANDY JASSY
1968–
American businessman, CEO and co-founder of Amazon Web Services

30-SECOND TEXT
Mark Steadman

Virtual cloud servers run programs as and when you need them.

CODE CONCEPTS

CODE CONCEPTS
GLOSSARY

abstraction In the context of programming environments, abstraction is about writing code that handles aspects of the appearance that the user might otherwise expect to be dealt with by their computer's own operating system – this is a way to make it easier to write programs that work on multiple systems.

algorithm The term for the mathematical aspect of a computer program; often an over-simplification. For example, Google is often described as having an algorithm in the singular, but many aspects go towards the system's ranking of websites.

API Application Programming Interface is a set of rules that allows developers on one project to build software that can communicate with another. Large firms use APIs to help smaller developers access their services (and in so doing encourage them to choose *their* system).

BASIC Beginners All Purpose Symbolic Instruction Code – a programming language created in 1964, which was many people's first experience of programming.

C One of the first programming languages, this is foundational for Python among others. As it is older, it is more useful for programming hardware than web apps. The more modern extension, C++, does have uses in computer games and simulations.

call To use a function.

cross-platform A piece of software or file that works on more than one type of computer system.

declare To allocate a space in the memory to store a variable (piece of data).

floating point A method of mathematical representation for real numbers that are especially large or small, which takes the form [significand] $\times$ [base] to the power of [exponent]: $2.5951 \times 10^4 = 25951$. You might also choose a limit on the number of digits in the significand to reduce the overall computational load on the computer – limit it to three decimal places and we would only record 2.595*104 (in code * = multiply).

GNU A free UNIX-like operating system and collection of free associated programs, produced in a project initiated by Richard Stallman while working at MIT. GNU stands for GNU's Not Unix to emphasize that it contains no UNIX code.

integer A whole number, or one that can be written without fractions – 1, 3, 10, 345 are all integers, but 3.45 is not.

Java The programming language associated with client-server applications thanks to its 'write-once, run anywhere' design.

JavaScript The most popular language for building interactive web content. There are also a number of extensions available. There is a risk that a browser will block some JavaScript if it thinks it is part of a pop-up or other security concern.

nested When one element is contained within another, just as a folder is contained within another folder on your computer's drive. Many languages allow nesting of instructions, too.

OpenGL A cross-platform API for rendering 2D and 3D graphics, which was transferred to non-profit management by Silicon Graphics in 2006. A replacement, Vulkan, has been available since 2016.

output Information that comes from the computer – it does not need to be printed or put on a disk; shown on screen counts.

pixel Short for picture element, this is the smallest unit of display on a computer's monitor (or in an image file).

RISC Reduced Instruction Set Computer – a processor design using fewer instructions, which can be operated more quickly.

SSD Solid State Drive (faster data storage without moving parts).

statement A single line of code correctly written that makes a command.

UNIX Trademarked operating system derived from internal work at AT&T then licensed to others.

Unreal Engine Originally written for first-person game *Unreal*, this library of code to help design and run games has been made available to other developers for a royalty.

virtual machine A simulation of a computer running on another computer, used either to sell commoditized computer power, or to use software you couldn't otherwise use on your system.

BINARY & BITS

the 30-second code

There is quite a difference

between a string of 1s and 0s and, say, a full-colour photograph. The 1s and 0s themselves are a representation – in the processor they will be represented by live or unpowered circuits. To represent a photograph, however, an agreed system, or format, is required. Typically a format will begin by establishing the basics (the size of the picture), before moving into describing each part consecutively. In a photograph these will be pixels, and the brightness of each will be represented by a number. If the pixel was '1-bit', that would mean only two possible settings for each pixel, 1 or 0, so a pure monochrome image – 0 meaning black, 1 meaning white. But if it were 8-bit (one byte is eight bits), that would offer up to 256 shades – 00000000 to 11111111, which is easier to think of as 2 to the power of 8 (2^8). If you want a colour image, it's possible to represent most colours with shades of red, green and blue (it's called additive colour, and 100 per cent of each equals white), so if you had eight bits (8 binary digits) times three for each pixel, you'd have $(2*2*2*2*2*2*2*2)*3 = 16.8$ million possible shades.

RELATED TOPICS
See also
VARIABLES
page 68

UNICODE
page 126

3-SECOND BIOGRAPHY
GOTTFRIED WILHELM VON LEIBNIZ
1646–1716
One of the most significant mathematicians, logicians and natural philosophers of the Enlightenment, and the first to describe a mechanical calculator

30-SECOND TEXT
Adam Juniper

3-SECOND BIT
A bit is the most basic binary unit of data that computers use, and a byte is eight bits.

3-MINUTE BYTE
When designing computers, it's possible to handle multiple bits at once, allowing larger numbers to be processed at any one time and making the machine faster. The world has marched on from 2-bit machines, through an era of 8-bit, 16-bit, 32-bit and now, usually, 64-bit. The speed of this change makes using code (that stays the same) even more essential.

A full colour photograph is made of up pixels which are represented by binary digits.

DATA TYPES

the 30-second code

3-SECOND BIT
In many languages, computers prefer to ascribe a type to a piece of data, like a number or string; this tells them how to use it.

3-MINUTE BYTE
Unlike other data types, Booleans hold one of only two possible values: true or false. Booleans control the flow of code: their values determine paths through if-then-else blocks and whether or not to continue repeating a loop. When you add a new 5K time to your running app, the code may use Booleans to store whether you ran a personal best and determine if you earned a new achievement.

In programming, we have to know and be specific about the types of data we are dealing with so we can work with them. Why? Well, if we have a long sequence of digits, such as 15554377439, how can we tell whether it's an indication of quantity, or a phone number? When we specify a data type for a variable, for example when we write code using a high-level programming language, we are telling the compiler or interpreter how much memory to allocate for it, what values can be stored in the variable's memory location and which kind of operations it should allow to be performed on the variable. So, if our long sequence of digits is a number, we can perform calculations on it. If, however, it is a string, the digits are treated as a set of characters. A string is what's known as a composite type, along with arrays (a list of items that could be mixed, for example, words and numbers) and objects (such as a telephone directory where data is paired up, in this case names and telephone numbers). Primitive data types are the building blocks of composite types and include numbers (integers and floating point), characters (including letters, digits, symbols and punctuation) and Booleans.

RELATED TOPICS
See also
VARIABLES
page 68

IF-THEN-ELSE: CONDITIONAL STATEMENTS
page 70

LOOPS & ITERATIONS
page 72

30-SECOND TEXT
Suze Shardlow

A piece of data, like a number or string, can be specified as a type to tell computers how to use it.

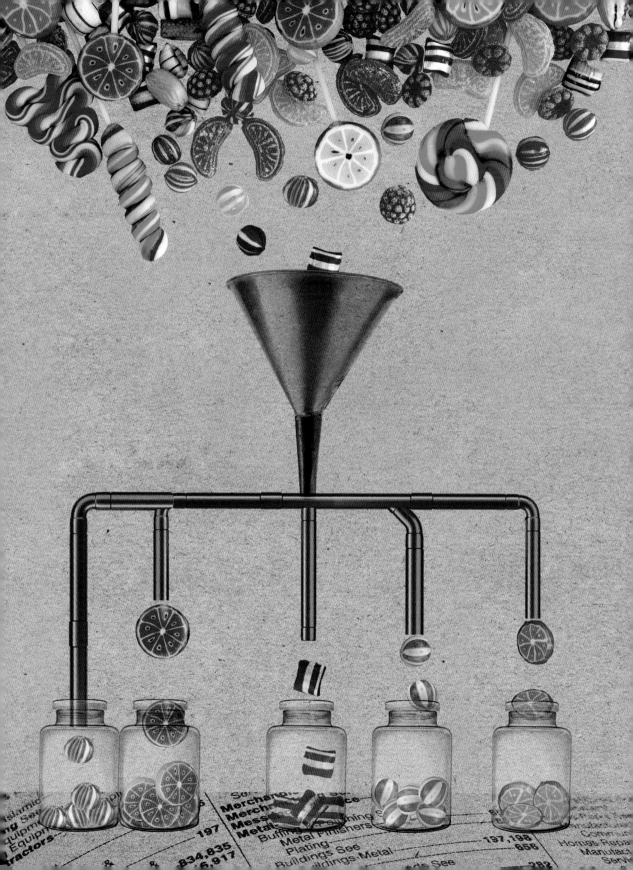

28 December 1969
Born in Helsinki, Finland

1988
Attends the University of Helsinki

1991
The first public prototypes of Linux are released

1993
Meets his future wife and karate champion Tove Monni at an introductory computer lab course he was running

1994
Version 1.0 of Linux is publicly released on 14 March

1996
A 4.6-km (2.9-mile) diameter asteroid – 9793 Torvalds – is named in his honour

1997
Moves to California to work for Transmeta, a semiconductor company

1999
Named by the *MIT Technology Review* as one of the world's top innovators under 35

1999
Gifted shares by Red Hat and VA Linux and their value briefly surpasses $20 million

2003
Moves to the Open Source Development Labs (now part of the Linux Foundation)

2010
Naturalized as an American citizen

2012
Declared one of the two winners of the €1 million Millennium Technology Prize

2018
Announces a period of time off in order to seek 'assistance on how to understand people's emotions and respond appropriately'

LINUS TORVALDS

Finnish-American Linus Benedict Torvalds showed an interest in programming as early as age 11, in 1981, quickly moving from BASIC to directly accessing his Commodore VIC-20's 6502 CPU via machine code. In 1988 he attended the University of Helsinki, where his parents had been campus radicals in the 1960s, and didn't leave until 1996, by which time he'd not only gained a master's degree in computer science but had also had an impact on computing the world over.

He surrendered almost his entire second year at university to Finland's compulsory military service, but did find the time to read about MINIX, a stripped-down version of UNIX, so when he actually encountered UNIX in 1990 the idea of altering the operating system was already in his mind and – significantly – he had been irritated by the licensing terms of MINIX. His MSc thesis was called 'Linus: A Portable Operating System'. UNIX's licensing history was already quite complex, having originally been pried away from AT&T division Bell Laboratories by a US anti-trust judgment, then ensnared again when AT&T divested itself of Bell Laboratories. A project called GNU had been attempting to build a complete free computer system, based on UNIX, since 1984. Torvalds has said he wouldn't have created his own system if GNU had been going better in 1991, but in January that year he began work on his version, Linux, and – after encountering the GNU project later that year – released the kernel (core) of the operating system under the GNU's legal license.

Now Torvalds owns the Linux trademark through his company, Linux Mark Institute (LMI), and works full-time on improving Linux thanks to sponsorship from the Linux Foundation. He has disagreed with other developers more than once on the Linux developers' mailing list, using pretty colourful language, and described himself a 'really unpleasant person', even briefly stepping down from active work on the kernel following an enquiry by *The New Yorker* in 2018.

Adam Juniper

DATA STRUCTURES: ARRAYS

the 30-second code

3-SECOND BIT
Arrays usually contain a
number of items of the
same type, stored at
adjacent memory locations.
We predetermine how
many elements we are
storing.

3-MINUTE BYTE
It's crucial to plan how
much we need to store in
our arrays. If we allocate
too much space, we use
memory inefficiently. If
we need to store more than
we originally declared, the
remedy is time-consuming:
we create a new array of
the correct length and copy
everything into it. Not so
bad if we have 20 songs
on a playlist, but slow if
we're tracking worldwide
ticket sales.

Just as its meaning in English, an
array in coding is a range of items of a certain
type. It's a special kind of variable that allows us
to store more than one piece of information. In
its simplest form, it could be a collection of
words grouped as strings, for example, a list of
songs in your band's repertoire. Arrays can
contain other data types (such as integers) or
data structures (such as other arrays and
objects). When we declare an array, we may
specify the type and maximum number of
elements it will hold. The system then allocates
adjacent blocks of memory for those items,
which allows us to find and retrieve existing
ones or add new ones quickly. We can access
each element in an array using its position
(index). So if we're playing a short set, we can
print out the first three songs, or if we're
playing a wedding we can print the first 20
songs. If we learn a new song we can insert it
into our repertoire array. We can remove songs
we are bored of. If they were at the beginning
or in the middle of the array, everything shifts
to the left to close the gap, thereby preserving
the contiguity.

RELATED TOPICS
See also
BINARY & BITS
page 60

DATA TYPES
page 62

VARIABLES
page 68

3-SECOND BIOGRAPHY
JOHN VON NEUMANN
1903–57
Hungarian-American polymath
who wrote the first array
sorting program, merge sort

30-SECOND TEXT
Suze Shardlow

*Arrays allow us to store
more than one piece of
information, such as a
list of songs.*

CLASSICS and VARIETIES

ROCK and ROLL

C1 D1
C2 D2
C3 D3
C4 D4
C5 D5
C6 D6
C7 D7
C8 D8
C9 D9

E1 F1
E2 F2
E3 F3
E4 F4
E5 F5
E6 F6
7 F7
8 F8
E9 F9

A B C D E F G H J K
1 2 3 4 5 6 7 8 9 10

VARIABLES

the 30-second code

We use variables in programming

to give us an easy way of labelling – and, therefore, recalling and manipulating – memory locations in which we store pieces of information. For example, our program might ask the user for their name and location. When the user submits these pieces of information, we can assign these values to named variables: currentUser = 'Suze' and currentUserLocation = 'Europe'. The computer stores these values in the memory locations associated with each variable. This allows us to greet the user by name, with a salutation appropriate to the time of day where they are. When declaring a variable, we can decide whether or not its value can be modified. We also need to decide the scope of the variable: where it can be seen and used in the program. Some variables have a global scope, so they can be used anywhere in the code. Others have a scope that is limited to a specific code block. For example, currentTime may only exist in a function where you are determining whether it's morning or evening in the user's time zone. In addition to a name and value, variables in most programming languages also have types. For example, a variable whose type is 'integer' can hold whole number values.

3-SECOND BIT
Variables associate a meaningful name with a memory location where we can store information that our program needs.

3-MINUTE BYTE
Readability is important when producing code. Therefore, we should give our variables meaningful names, such as currentUser, so anyone working on the code base can understand what the software is doing. We can also use variables to substitute for numbers in calculations. For example, if we have a set of 5K race times, we can store the fastest in a variable named personalBest and compare other race times to it.

RELATED TOPICS
See also
BINARY & BITS
page 60

DATA TYPES
page 62

DATA STRUCTURES: ARRAYS
page 66

30-SECOND TEXT
Suze Shardlow

Variables offer a convenient way of labelling memory locations for pieces of information, such as name, time and location.

IF-THEN-ELSE: CONDITIONAL STATEMENTS

the 30-second code

Unless a program takes no

inputs, in which case it might not do much, it will need to select courses of action based on the inputs we give it. Conditional statements are crucial building blocks of algorithms and allow us to set out what the computer must do if certain things are true. Without conditional statements, we may not get the desired result. Nothing may happen, everything may happen or the wrong things may happen. For example, we want to order a takeaway. Our first choice is chicken and chips, so if it's true that that's available then we will buy that. Otherwise, we will look to see if it's true that fish and chips are available. If we can't buy that then we will look for pizza. If this is also unavailable then we buy nothing and we eat something from the freezer. If we don't define these statements, we limit our options. However, by putting these foods in order, we limit our options by purchasing the first available meal. We can visualize this block of code using a flow chart. Conditional statements mean we can skip to different parts of a program depending on the scenario we face, as opposed to running unnecessary code.

RELATED TOPICS
See also
LOOPS & ITERATIONS
page 72

FUNCTIONS
page 76

30-SECOND TEXT
Suze Shardlow

3-SECOND BIT
IF we have chicken in the fridge **THEN** we'll make that for dinner, **ELSE** we'll phone for a pizza.

3-MINUTE BYTE
We can use conditional statements to tell the computer to move to a different part of the program. This can mean moving backwards as well as forwards. Because they check to see whether something is true before executing more code, conditional statements form the basis of loops and iterations: where the program goes back and repeats an action if a certain condition has not been met.

Conditional statements are crucial building blocks to help programs achieve desired results.

LOOPS & ITERATIONS

the 30-second code

3-SECOND BIT
Loops enable us to perform repetitive processes consistently without having to duplicate our code.

3-MINUTE BYTE
We can tell a loop to stop at a certain point. But what if we don't? Then we have an infinite loop. Often, these will crash your program. However, sometimes we want iterations to continue indefinitely. For example, if we program our central heating to come on at certain times each day, we want the sequence in that loop to keep iterating for as long as the program is running.

Coding is all about automating actions to create efficiencies. Even the smallest or simplest programs have loops built in, so we can repeatedly run the same code without having to write it out again. For example, say we are training for a half marathon and we are writing an app to track how many times we have been for a run. If we want to see our run details on the app's home page, we need some code that looks at our stored data, picks out a run date and distance and prints it. To get a list of runs, we need to put a loop around that code so when the program prints the first run, it goes back to find and print the next, and so on. Unless we want an infinite loop, we tell loops to continue either until they've operated on all the data in a set, or for a defined number of iterations, or until a condition is met. So you can either print all the runs you've ever done, only print the ten most recent runs or keep printing them until the total distance run is 100 km (62 miles).

RELATED TOPICS
See also
IF-THEN-ELSE: CONDITIONAL STATEMENTS
page 70

FUNCTIONS
page 76

MAKING CODE PORTABLE
page 78

30-SECOND TEXT
Suze Shardlow

Putting loops around codes allows us to look back at our stored data and pick out run dates and distances.

11 August 1950
Born in San Jose,
California, USA

1969
Expelled from the
University of Colorado,
Boulder

1971
Transfers to University of
California, Berkeley;
creates a computer called
'Cream Soda' with friend
Bill Fernandez

1975
Tests the first working
Apple 1 prototype

1976
Jobs and Wozniak form
the Apple Computer
Company; later that year
former Intel staffer Mike
Markkula provides
significant investment

1977
Introduces the Apple II at
the West Coast Computer
Faire (and in *Byte*
magazine)

1980
Apple goes public,
making both founders
millionaires

1981
Wozniak crashes a plane
with his then fiancée and
two friends on board

1985
Awarded USA National
Medal of Technology

1986
Gives his name to the
'Wozzie Awards' for
innovation

1987
Wozniak's own
company creates the first
programmable universal
remote control

2011
Apple supplants Exxon
Mobil as the largest
company in the world

2015
Depicted by Seth Rogen
in the Danny Boyle /
Aaron Sorkin *Steve Jobs*
movie

STEVE WOZNIAK

Steve Wozniak is an American electronics engineer and programmer best known for co-founding Apple, though money seems to have been a secondary motivation. At college he was introduced to Steve Jobs and they quickly became friends owing to a shared interest in electronics and pranks. Jobs, though, was somewhat more commercial minded. When, in 1971, 'Woz' built a little blue box that helped students circumvent the high cost of long-distance phone calls, it was Jobs who set about selling the gadget at $150 a piece.

Two years later, Jobs was working at Atari and needed help on a technical project. The firm promised him a $100 bonus for every chip he was able to eliminate from the *Breakout* arcade unit. Jobs enlisted Wozniak, promising him half the bonus. Woz eliminated 50 chips, but instead of giving Woz $2,500, Jobs lied and told him Atari only gave him $700, so handed over just $350, a fact Woz didn't discover for a decade.

By 1975 Woz and Jobs were both working at Hewlett-Packard (HP), and Wozniak – inspired by friends in the Palo Alto Homebrew Computer Club – created a computer from parts. When his employers turned it down, he and Jobs sold their own possessions to fund the first batch of circuit boards of what they called the 'Apple 1'. Eventually around 200 units of the bare-board design were sold to hobbyists for $500 each, but a month later Apple Inc. was founded and Wozniak began work on the Apple II. Jobs wanted to keep costs down, but Woz threatened to walk off the job unless the machine had eight expansion slots. Woz won, and, as it transpired, the 1977 machine was hugely successful.

Although Wozniak also helped with the early Macintosh, his dedication to the Apple II's large installed user base probably kept Apple afloat. In 1981 Woz crashed a light aircraft, taking him away from computers for some time (though he did try establishing rock-and-tech festivals). In 1983 he returned to Apple as an engineer, avoiding management before eventually leaving again and selling most of his stock in 1985. He is now known for his tech-leaning philanthropy, such as helping to found the Electronic Frontier Foundation, Silicon Valley Comic Con and Woz U education service.

Adam Juniper

FUNCTIONS
the 30-second code

RELATED TOPICS
See also
VARIABLES
page 68

LOOPS & ITERATIONS
page 72

3-SECOND BIT
A function has a single purpose, which should not overlap with any other function, and needs a unique name, ideally describing its role (such as validateMove).

3-MINUTE BYTE
Generally, but not always (it depends on the language), functions can be nested inside other functions. So a function that deals with sorting cats by age (sortCatsByAge) can contain a function to calculate a cat's age (calculateCatsAge) given its date of birth. The first function, sortCatsByAge, then takes the output of the nested function, calculateCatsAge, to sort the cats into ascending order by age.

A popular coding mantra is DRY:
Don't Repeat Yourself. Large programs will often need to execute the same instructions over and over. However, code ideally needs to be readable and maintainable. Having multiple copies of the same lines of code at different points in a program means that any changes to that code need to be made to every occurrence. To save us rewriting blocks of code and keep them manageable, we enclose them within functions (or subroutines). Each function has a name which we use to 'call' (use) it. The functions can then be called each time we need to use them. The output of a function is a piece of information produced by running the code contained in the function in the context of the arguments, or parameters, we pass into it. One use of a function might be to reset a board so the player can start a new game; another function could calculate whether the player has made a valid move. Any variables declared within a function cannot be accessed outside the function. Breaking code into functions allows us as programmers to test individual pieces of code independently of each other. This means we can speed up development as we can more easily define and test the scope of change.

3-SECOND BIOGRAPHIES
JOHN MAUCHLY
1907–80
American physicist who co-designed the ENIAC – the first programmable electronic computer – and, in early 1947, discussed the simplicity of coding functions (or subroutines as they used to be known)

KAY MCNULTY
1921–2006
One of the six original programmers of the ENIAC who developed the use of functions to help calculate missile trajectories

30-SECOND TEXT
Suze Shardlow

Functions are used to reset a board, to start a new game, or to calculate if a player has made a valid move.

MAKING CODE PORTABLE

the 30-second code

Humankind has long sought to make things easier to take with them. Making code portable isn't about reducing size and weight – it is about making it work universally. Different processors have different instructions, so portability needs to be solved by compiling appropriate programs. Ideally, the same piece of code could simply be written in a cross-platform language (Java, C, C++ under certain circumstances) and compiled for each different computer it is run on. In practice, there are obstacles – different operating systems handle things differently. To write an app for Mac and PC, one can choose to use the individual system's libraries as little as possible, perhaps even writing their own code for features that they might be able to hand off to the operating system's built-in features otherwise (called 'abstraction'). The result may stray further from either computer's style guide, but the code will be less affected by a change affecting one or other platform. Code libraries and functions can provide solutions; the main program could take advantage of a specific library to load or save a file on its host computer. When you compile the code into a working application (done on each system) swap the relevant load/save library. Many libraries, such as OpenGL, emphasize their cross-platform credentials.

RELATED TOPICS
See also
CODE LIBRARIES
page 52

FUNCTIONS
page 76

3-SECOND BIOGRAPHY
TIM SWEENEY
1970–
American programmer and CEO who created and sold game-creation tools, famously the engine behind 1998 success *Unreal*

30-SECOND TEXT
Adam Juniper

3-SECOND BIT
The same language can work on many computers, but there will still be conflicts to address.

3-MINUTE BYTE
A common solution to portability is writing web applications in JavaScript (not the same thing as Java). For security, these programs have restricted access to the computer they are run on, but thanks to their nature are cross-platform. While JavaScript began as a way of extending the Web, it's also possible to abstract JavaScript to a local virtual machine.

Making code portable is about making it work universally across different programs.

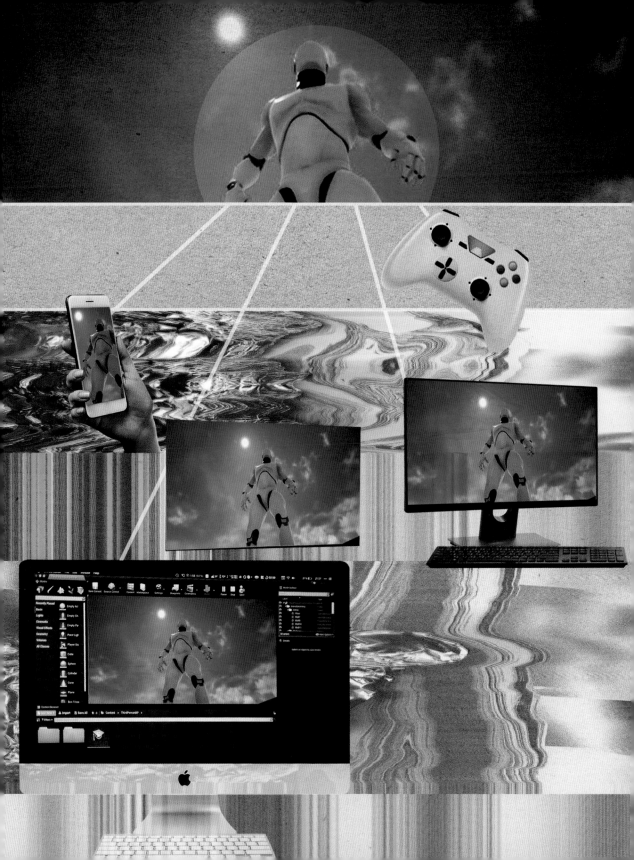

BUFFERING & CACHES

the 30-second code

3-SECOND BIT

A cache evens out the flow of data between systems; caches are about speed, buffers about flow.

3-MINUTE BYTE

Hardware caches, such as those in a CPU, are managed by the hardware, but there are a number of levels of software cache that might need to be guided by code. Accessing disks by a hierarchy of speed (SSD, hard drive, remote drive) and using each as a tiered cache is effective.

For a train, a buffer represents the end of the line. If you're trying to stream video, it can represent an irksome delay. But what is it, and is it different from a cache? The answer is that they both represent a store of data designed to ease the flow from one place to another. Imagine pouring water from a jug into a bucket with a shaky hand – it would all arrive in the bucket, but perhaps in splashes. A funnel could solve this – assuming the right size tube, the drops would instead fall randomly into the wide funnel top but flow out in an even stream down the narrow tube. A buffer and a cache both use memory to achieve this effect, but the difference is that a buffer is about delivery – by the end of the feed, all of the data will go through a buffer, whereas a cache is only there if needed for efficiency. A processor chip might have a dedicated piece of fast memory, but if the instructions aren't coming quickly enough to need it, they'll go straight into the processor. Caching is also common online – a web page may be cached at many points nearer the user than the host server. When coding these, a developer must deploy good 'policies' to tell the system when to refresh its cached file.

RELATED TOPICS

See also
ASSEMBLY LANGUAGE
page 40

EVENTUAL CONSISTENCY
page 82

3-SECOND BIOGRAPHY
JOHN COCKE
1925–2002
American computer scientist who worked on the IBM 801 Fast Processor project, the first implementing split caches, in 1975, and considered 'the Father of RISC'

30-SECOND TEXT
Adam Juniper

Buffers and caches represent a store of data designed to ease the flow from one place to another.

EVENTUAL CONSISTENCY

the 30-second code

3-SECOND BIT
Large-scale databases can track a single number using multiple computers and parallelism.

3-MINUTE BYTE
Eventual consistency works if there are enough servers to ensure the load on the main database can still, effectively, be a single thread. For that reason, some software designers also know it as 'optimistic replication', which emphasizes the point that taking data from the main database (or a recent cache) is adopting an 'It'll be fine in the end' approach rather than seeking scientific accuracy.

In the world of social media, nearly everything is counted. If you watch those numbers (views on YouTube, likes on Twitter and so on) you might find that they don't just climb up at a rational rate. Check something on your phone a moment after you do on your computer and the likes might have dropped by tens of thousands, but it's not (necessarily) because people have hit 'unlike'. This is a common example of multi-threading (on a very grand scale). A traditional program – one instruction after another – is a single 'thread', but big sites will have many of these happening at once, on multiple machines. Sometimes a number is so important that the system must be built around a single, absolutely accurate thread (if you're selling a finite product), but for 'likes', many interim servers can be counting in their own threads before sending on a total to be added together at a central thread. At any one time the central figure might be a little out, but, eventually, it'll be accurate. The like count is also stored in a cache on the interim servers that send it out, so the number you get depends when the cache updated itself.

RELATED TOPICS
See also
DATA STRUCTURES: ARRAYS
page 66

VARIABLES
page 68

BUFFERING & CACHES
page 80

3-SECOND BIOGRAPHY
WERNER VOGELS
1958–
Dutch-born Chief Technology Officer of Amazon, known for creating distributed computing platform Amazon Web Services (AWS) and writing on eventual consistency

30-SECOND TEXT
Adam Juniper

For 'likes', many interim servers can be counting their own threads.

WHAT CODERS DO

Ada A programming language named in Ada Lovelace's honour.

break point A point in a program at which it stops (breaks out of the sequence of performing instructions, back to awaiting a command).

computer science This is the academic field that relates to computers; it has its roots in mathematics, so is a broader subject than learning a single programming language.

console A text-only interface to a computer, for example, Win32 console (Windows) or Terminal (Mac). These can be useful for seeing exactly which steps the computer is taking, since they're printed on to the screen in sequence, creating a log.

CSS file Cascade Style Sheet – a file related to HTML that provides stylistic choices such as fonts and colours to avoid repetition.

event Much new code is event-driven – a bit of the program that is there waiting for something to happen (a button to be pressed) before it gets to work.

flag A bit of information that has an on/off value (likely written as a 1/0 value). As opposed to an Error flag, indicating something unusual.

HTML Hypertext Markup Language – the language for programming web pages, which uses codes such as <B> to start bold and </B> to end a bold section.

HTTP Hypertext Transfer Protocol – the language computers use to share web pages (a means of universal addressing of HTML files).

hypertext Text with links that can be used to click through to another page of text, such as a web page.

internet The internet refers to the wider connection that developed from Arpanet. At the top there is an application layer (for example, the World Wide Web or email), and the data travels over a transport layer (for example, TCP) and the internet layer (IP).

JavaScript The most popular language for building interactive web content. There are also a number of extensions available. There is a risk that a browser will block some JavaScript if it thinks it is part of a pop-up or other security concern.

metadata Related data to explain content, for example, the date on a photo.

open-source code A program in which the original non-compiled code is available to be looked at / used by others, either for free or for a license payment.

parse To analyse a string or text into its component parts so it can be understood; you may need to do this to an input, and the computer will do it to your code.

PHP A language largely used for server-side development, but slipping behind Python and JavaScript (as opposed to Java).

Python A high-level, object-orientated interpreted programming language first released in 1991, Python is designed to make code easy to read with space around the characters. Has integrations with C and C++.

relational database A database arranged like a (potentially giant) spreadsheet, each entry on a row with the first column, the 'key', holding a unique ID for each entry, and making it easy to find related data points.

Ruby A language that provided a framework for web applications and is still used for some, though Python, PHP and JavaScript have all overtaken it.

run time The phase in a program's life when it is being run on a computer's CPU.

run-time error An error detected while running the program on the computer's CPU, as opposed to one detected by the compiler (that is, when the program is written but before it is prepared to be run).

SQL Structured Query Language – a declarative programming language that allows accessing data without having to describe the method (leaving that to the server).

World Wide Web The World Wide Web is a platform (now the dominant one) for publishing content online, but it is just one of several systems that use the internet (known as application layers). Others are email, FTP, Telnet.

WYSIWYG What You See Is What You Get – software that allows you to edit something close to the finished product.

USER INTERFACE & USER EXPERIENCE

the 30-second code

3-SECOND BIT
Whether we're working on a website, a mobile app or a console game, the user interface and experience will form part of its key to success.

3-MINUTE BYTE
In one of the test versions of Apple's iPhone operating system from 2017, if you quickly tapped 1+2+3 in the calculator app, you might see the result 24. This is because each button carried a short animation to indicate when it had been pressed, but while the animation was playing the button was disabled. This meant the app interpreted 1+2+3 as 1+23. (The bug was quickly fixed, and never made it to the general public.)

The user interface (UI) is the thing the user (website visitor, device owner or player) sees when they interact with our software. This is a major part of the success of your creation, and often takes time, experimentation and repetition to get right. It might also evolve and change as trends in design come and go. It is part of user experience (UX), which also affects how the user feels when using the software. A user interface might have a number of beautiful animations that transition a user from one part of the application to another, but if they interfere with how the app works, this creates a bad user experience, and can lead to bigger problems. A good way to consider how you can improve a user interface is to imagine someone incredibly busy using your application. Does the space between buttons cause them to have to drag their mouse further than they need to? Can you include some keyboard shortcuts that would make a repetitive task easier? Does the contrast between the text and the background make information harder to read on a phone on a sunny day? Or, in the case of Apple's bug, are elements of the UI interfering with core functions of the app? These are all questions that someone might consider when crafting a piece of software people really want to use.

RELATED TOPICS
See also
SCALING & PSEUDOCODE
page 106

UNICODE
page 126

3-SECOND BIOGRAPHY
DOUGLAS ENGELBART
1925–2013
American inventor of the computer mouse and the concept of clickable text (hyperlinks), which he first demonstrated in 1968

30-SECOND TEXT
Mark Steadman

The effectiveness of user interface and experience can determine the success of your creation.

8 June 1955
Born in London, England

1969–73
Attends school near UK's busiest railway station, Clapham Junction

1973–76
Attends The Queen's College, Oxford, earning a first-class degree in physics

1976
Works as a telecommunications engineer

1980
Proposes a hypertext system at CERN during a brief consultancy

1981–4
Works on computer networking for a printing and scanning company

1984
Takes up a fellowship at CERN

1989
Proposes the World Wide Web at CERN

1990
On 20 December, publishes the first website (info.cern.ch)

1994
Founds W3C at Massachusetts Institute of Technology (MIT), which would go on to be the main standards organization for the Web

2004
Becomes a professor at the University of Southampton working on the Semantic Web project, a plan to make web pages machine-readable

2004
Knighted by Queen Elizabeth II 'for services to the global development of the internet'

2007
Appointed to the Order of Merit

2016
Receives the Association for Computing Machinery (ACM) Turing Award, considered the 'Nobel Prize of Computing'

TIM BERNERS-LEE

Oxford University graduate

Sir Tim Berners-Lee is a man often credited with having invented the internet. His true creation – the World Wide Web – lives upon the broader internet through the magic of code he wrote, and brought the technology to the masses.

Tim's parents met while working on the Manchester Ferranti Mark 1 – the first commercial computer. As a boy he was a keen trainspotter – this fed an interest in model railways, which ensured an interest in electronics. This he retained at university where, though he studied physics, he also bought electronic components and built a computer.

As a graduate, he went to Dorset to work for telecommunications firm Plessy, then software firm D. G. Nash where he wrote software for typesetting and a multi-tasking system, before becoming an independent consultant. In June 1980 he began a six-month stint at research centre CERN, where around 10,000 people were engaged in research, all working with different hardware and software. He proposed an information-sharing system, Enquire, which could be implemented on multiple systems.

Enquire was similar to a modern Wikipedia, but the system didn't succeed. The problem with Enquire's 'cards', Tim decided in 1984, when returning to CERN on a fellowship, was that other users couldn't create them (unless they had one already) or make external links, and that the database structure was taxing on processing power.

By 1989 the world had started to develop an interest in hypertext such as the HyperTies interactive encyclopaedia system (1983), Guide by Peter Brown (1982) or Apple's HyperCard (1987). For many the emphasis was encyclopaedia-like products, but at CERN Berners-Lee was more interested in simplicity and compatibility. He began work on 'WorldWideWeb'.

To create the Web, he needed specifications, which is where Hypertext Markup Language (HTML) came from. Made up of very few elements, many remain in web code today, the system was inspired by the existing structure of Standard Generalized Markup Language (SGML). Making the internet the conduit for hypertext, Berners-Lee's key innovation was Hypertext Transfer Protocol (HTTP). The work effectively nudged the community into creating a universal unique address for any file (page), known as a UDI, URL or URI.

The proposal, first written in March 1989, was described by his manager at CERN, Mike Sendall, as 'vague but exciting'. Interestingly for many used to the 'create' and 'surf' concepts, the original web browser also included a WYSIWYG authoring feature so users could create pages.

In 1994 Berners-Lee founded the World Wide Web Consortium (W3C), through which he could share his ideas freely, with no royalty charges, so the WWW wouldn't go the way of other SGML applications.

Adam Juniper

DATABASE OPERATION: CRUD

the 30-second code

If you want information to be saved when your application closes and then accessed again when you reopen it, you'll need a database. A database consists of a number of tables, like tabs in a spreadsheet document. Data can be linked between those tables, and sorted, filtered and changed by issuing the commands INSERT, SELECT, UPDATE or DELETE. When we talk informally about them, we substitute INSERT for 'create' and SELECT for 'read', hence the acronym 'CRUD'. Each item in our database (that is, each line in a spreadsheet) is called a record. Once a record is created in a database, it's saved to disk until deleted. You can create a single record, or lots of records at the same time. Each record usually has an incremental number associated to it (like the row number in a spreadsheet), which we call a primary key. You can access data records using the primary key, you can filter the data to find a specific row(s) matching your criteria, you can sort data in any direction and you can count the matching rows. UPDATE and DELETE work as you'd expect them to, SELECT can be used as a search tool. It's worth remembering that, at the basic level, replacing or deleting data does not back up the original content.

RELATED TOPICS
See also
DATA TYPES
page 62

DATA STRUCTURES: ARRAYS
page 66

3-SECOND BIOGRAPHY
EDGAR F. CODD
1923–2003
English computer scientist who came up with the relational database while working at IBM

30-SECOND TEXT
Mark Steadman

3-SECOND BIT
The basic act of creating, reading, organizing and deleting information on a database (like a spreadsheet) is known as CRUD.

3-MINUTE BYTE
Experts encourage people to use SQL as a declarative language (queries don't specify the method), though there are still some who insist on calling it procedural or semi-procedural. That MySQL can store procedures as subroutines seems to persuade some to categorize it this way (but we know they're wrong).

The relational model for database management was invented by Edgar F. Codd whilst working for IBM.

WEB DEVELOPMENT
the 30-second code

Websites are pieces of software that run on one or more servers (computers that send data when requested). It's often called 'the cloud'. The job of the web server is to handle requests from what is known as a 'client' (a web browser on a phone, for example) and issue a response. A user doesn't see that work, only the resulting message. That means that, if properly set up, the web server can handle secret information because only the specific client who asked will see it. It also means the server can do much more than the user ever sees, such as running programs to decide what to send to the client. This is called server-side web development. As well as static files, such as web pages, almost all websites use a database. Blogs store entries in a database and the blogger will have a password allowing them to get to the 'back end' to edit them. SQL is a language for addressing certain databases, which might be kept separately from web pages. Early sites simply sent HTML files on request, a bit like opening a document in Word. Now HTML pages will seek a CSS file (to tell them their font and styling), and might fill gaps from the database, or use scripts (mini-programs hidden in the page). None of this is seen by the client – they just see a finished page.

RELATED TOPICS
See also
RUNNING CODE IN
THE CLOUD
page 54

TIM BERNERS-LEE
page 90

DATABASE OPERATION: CRUD
page 92

END-TO-END ENCRYPTION
page 128

3-SECOND BIOGRAPHIES
RASMUS LERDORF
1968–
Danish-Canadian who co-authored the PHP scripting language and the Apache HTTP server

ROBERT MCCOOL
1973–
Original author of the NCSA HTTPd (later Apache) web server, helping make the Web dynamic

30-SECOND TEXT
Mark Steadman

Web servers handle requests and issue responses, with the user only seeing the resulting message.

3-SECOND BIT
Programming websites means understanding the difference between static content and dynamic, programmable elements.

3-MINUTE BYTE
Common languages for server-side development are PHP, Ruby, Python and JavaScript, and these instructions need to be performed on the server, which means you need to pay for the computing power that performs server-side tasks, including necessary 'resources' such as memory. JavaScript can also be run in the client's browser, which can be cheaper, but relies on the client having a suitable machine.

SCRIPTING

the 30-second code

RELATED TOPICS

See also
COMPILED CODE
page 48

Whereas we might think of a computer program as being in some way interactive, with the user asked at different stages to give information, a script usually takes a small amount of input, if any, and then runs a task, or a number of tasks, in a linear fashion. Scripts are meant to do one particular job in a way that is easily repeated. For example, let's say you're a wedding photographer, you have a card full of photos from a shoot, and you want to organize them on your computer. You could click and drag each, one after the other, to the right folder and rename to include the time and location, or you could create a script – a program that acts a bit like a single user. A script can look at the metadata on the photos and construct a filename based on the data. It loops through each photo on the card, looking at the file's timestamp to find out when the photo was taken, then it examines each file's metadata to pull out the coordinates of the location the photo was taken. The script calls an online service to turn those coordinates into a human-readable place name.

30-SECOND TEXT
Mark Steadman

3-SECOND BIT
A script is the perfect work-experience employee, handling a mindless repetitive computing task in the form of simple instructions.

3-MINUTE BYTE
Unlike computer programs, scripts don't need to be compiled, which means you can run them on any computer that understands that language. Some applications have scripting tools (including photographers' favourite Photoshop). Ruby, Python and JavaScript are three common scripting languages, which are easy to read, and work across different computing platforms, including phones and tablets.

Scripts run repetitive tasks in a linear fashion using only a small amount of input.

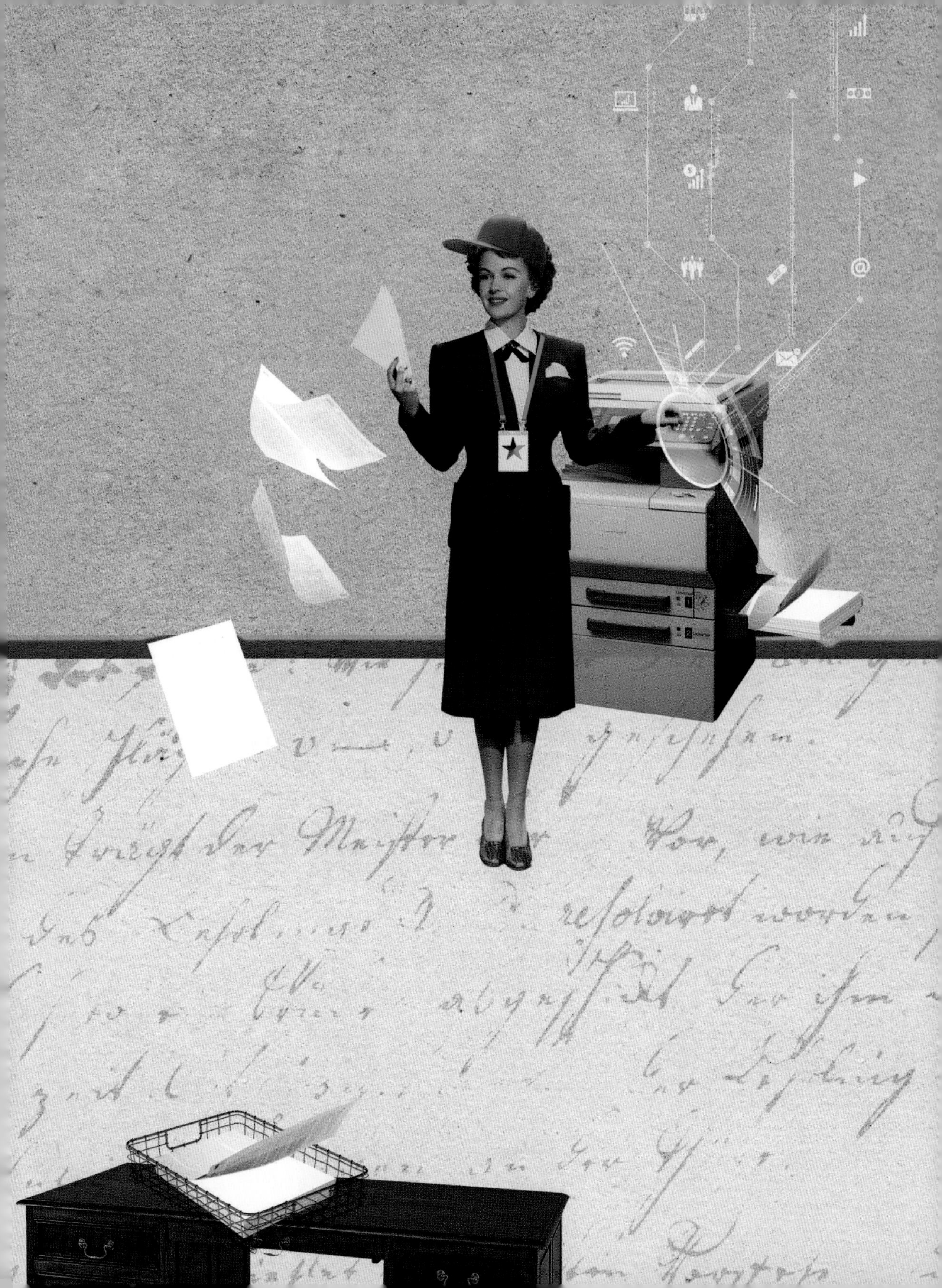

ENGINEERING

the 30-second code

Understanding code can open up paths in terms of a career, but that gateway seems to be accompanied by some very confusing signposting. People who work with code seem to employ a number of different titles – but what do they mean? While there is no absolute, the name 'coder' is typically applied to someone early in their career who is engaged in generating specific pieces of code – equivalent to a junior copywriter (indeed they might be called a 'junior programmer'). More experience brings the title 'developer' or 'programmer' and implies a greater appreciation for the whole of the project being undertaken, like a site manager in a building job. The title of 'engineer' suggests a more architectural role, developing the plans that the developers and coders need to follow. An engineer will need an understanding of the purpose of their project and any external resources it might connect to. The truth is there is a huge potential for overlap, not least because, at one, end the world of software is still full of self-starters who have taken on every role, while giant firms create their own additional titles (including, as it happens, 'software architect').

RELATED TOPICS
See also
DEBUGGING
page 104

ALGORITHMS
page 112

3-SECOND BIT
Titles in programming roles are loosely defined, but typically engineer is the broadest role.

3-MINUTE BYTE
When looking at courses, computer science as a subject is more academic and more mechanical than software engineering, which is more career-based. Computer science demands strong mathematics (algebra is involved in algorithm design) but leaves students with a broader understanding of the technology, especially hardware. Modern courses also include classes in areas such as computing ethics and patents.

3-SECOND BIOGRAPHY
SIR MAURICE
VINCENT WILKES
1913–2010
British computer scientist who designed an early electronic computer and head of the world's first course in computer science at Cambridge University

30-SECOND TEXT
Mark Steadman

Engineers have a more architectural coding role.

AGILE DEVELOPMENT & THE SCRUM

the 30-second code

RELATED TOPICS
See also
WEB DEVELOPMENT
page 94

ENGINEERING
page 98

Scrum is a working process that emerged to replace a programming model known as 'waterfall', in which a project was planned, built, tested, reviewed and finally deployed in sequence. This could be potentially time-consuming and the market may well have moved on in that time. In the 1970s the principle of adaptive software development emerged, a more iterative approach that allowed working on small elements and testing. This began to be formalized under various names in the 1990s, one of which was Scrum, in 1995. The principle of a Scrum project was that the wider project was divided into incremental releases called 'sprints', each of which was planned for only enough time before work could begin on a build. Each sprint ends with a 'potentially shippable product'. Scrum needs a 'product owner', who defines the required features (known as the 'product backlog'), a 'Scrum master', who leads the team, and a team who can act as developers or testers as required, tackling the work in small units called 'user stories'. In 2001, 17 developers behind the wave of lightweight development methods published the *Manifesto for Agile Software Development*, listing principles including 'early and continuous development', 'delivering working software frequently' and 'close, daily cooperation'.

3-SECOND BIT
Agile development, of which Scrum is a method, encourages regular delivery of working versions.

3-MINUTE BYTE
In 2015, Microsoft CEO Satya Nadella said 'every business today will become a software business', and for many that is now true. The Agile approach is now merging with traditional corporate management with its emphasis on business goals and strategy. The upshot is developers are often required to enable Value Stream Management (VSM) – tracking the delivery of value against the original request.

3-SECOND BIOGRAPHY
JIM HIGHSMITH
1945–
American software engineer who spent 25 years as an IT manager and developer, before writing *Adaptive Software Development* (2000); wrote the foreword to the Agile manifesto

30-SECOND TEXT
Adam Juniper

Scrum is a method of agile development, dividing wider projects into incremental 'sprints'.

HACKING

the 30-second code

You don't need to know about computers to have encountered hackers, but it's fair to say that Hollywood (not to mention security policy authors) treat the word somewhat flexibly. The attempt to gain unauthorized access to computer systems is more accurately known as 'security hacking', and there are three notable sub-groups: white-hat (those who aim to discover vulnerabilities so they can be repaired), black-hat (also known as 'crackers', this group is looking to steal and exploit data for personal gain) and grey-hat (those who might be described as hobbyists – likely not seeking financial gain, but probably still breaking the law). Programming and technology enthusiasts might consider themselves part of 'hacker culture' without necessarily engaging in any security hacking. These 'hackers' have a passionate interest in systems for the sheer fun of it, as opposed to users who need only the basic commands to achieve their goals. The culture first emerged in the 1960s on college campuses, and as time moved on it became more self-conscious, creating the Jargon File in 1973 (a glossary of programmers' slang) and *GNU Manifesto* in 1985 (the goal of a free computer operating system). Cultural hackers are more homogenized since internet communication, but still support freedom of information.

RELATED TOPICS
See also
LINUS TORVALDS
page 64

STEVE WOZNIAK
page 74

END-TO-END ENCRYPTION
page 128

3-SECOND BIT
There is some overlap between security hacking and legitimately testing networked systems, which coders might well be expected to work on.

3-MINUTE BYTE
Cultural hacking is associated with a sense of humour or doing simply for the sake of doing rather than for profit. This can be expressed as 'hack value', and examples include using a dot matrix printer to produce musical notes. Linux creator Linus Torvalds, a hero of the hacker community, has said that in this way hacking incorporates the spirit of capitalism.

3-SECOND BIOGRAPHY
KEN THOMPSON
1943–
When collecting his Turing Award for pioneering work on UNIX and 'B' (the language that pre-dated C) in 1983, Thompson referenced the term 'Trojan Horse' in relation to a term now well established in computer security.

30-SECOND TEXT
Adam Juniper

Hackers come in various forms and guises.

DEBUGGING

the 30-second code

Problems in code are known as

bugs; correcting them is debugging. Since very little code works first time, much of coding is debugging, though there is a wide range of potential problems. Given how little time the authors gave the editors on this book, it might have a syntax error – the failure to use proper punctuation or grammar – but you'd likely be able to read through it and work out what was meant. A computer cannot, and will likely just stop. On the plus side, these can often be spotted automatically. Errors can also be generated from code that does not parse properly, and they're slightly harder to spot – the program will run but will not do what you hoped. Programming environments include tools to assist debugging, such as the console log or break points, which can be added to any line of code to check a value. Move the break point until you work out the point at which things go wrong. Programs also need to interact with cloud servers, and instruct those servers to talk to remote platforms. These servers keep a moment-by-moment event log, so if a program you write receives any error messages you'll be able to find it.

3-SECOND BIT
Debugging means working through code and identifying problems, developing a hypothesis for each issue and testing it until it is resolved, and moving on.

3-MINUTE BYTE
The first step to debugging is to clearly identify a serious bug and be able to reproduce the issue – what inputs cause it to appear? What steps? This helps identify which part of the code is to blame and that might be something written by a colleague or sourced from a code library. This is where asking team-mates and having open-source code to review are essential.

RELATED TOPICS
See also
GRACE HOPPER
page 44

COMPILED CODE
page 48

30-SECOND TEXT
Adam Juniper

Much of coding involves correcting problems in a process known as debugging.

SCALING & PSEUDOCODE

the 30-second code

A simple game such as Fizz Buzz can easily be tackled by a programmer, as the rules are simply defined and the game doesn't rely on any remote servers or other elements. However, a complex 3D game that has lots of animation, multiple characters moving around and interacting with the environment, realistic lighting and immersive sound, requires that work to be much more tightly defined. Each part of the game engine is handled by a different sub-team, headed by a project manager or a systems architect, who will then work with coders to write a specification for each part of the system before any lines of code are written. A step towards achieving this is 'pseudocode', which means writing the steps that need to be achieved in terse plain English, with just the detail that is needed to design and develop a new method for solving a problem on a whiteboard before anyone is assigned a programming task. There are many styles of pseudocode, which might be more or less like the author's preferred computer programming language. Some, such as Z-notation, are more mathematical. At the other end of the scale is Program Design Language (PDL), which uses no programming terms.

RELATED TOPICS
See also
THE FIZZBUZZ TEST
page 114

AGILE DEVELOPMENT
& THE SCRUM
page 100

3-SECOND BIOGRAPHIES
NIKLAUS WIRTH
1934–
Swiss computer scientist behind 'Wirth's Law' – as computers get faster, software gets slower. It is this that Christophe de Dinechin aims to resolve with XL

JEAN-RAYMOND ABRIAL
1938–
French computer scientist who developed Z-notation and B-Method while at the University of Oxford

30-SECOND TEXT
Mark Steadman

3-SECOND BIT
Writing software in 'real' English doesn't help computers read it, but can give a team a starting point they can explain to a client.

3-MINUTE BYTE
XL ('eXtensible Language') is a real computer programming language designed specifically to support 'concept programming' (in which developers turn concepts into code by concentrating on the difference between what is in their mind and what ends up in code). Development on it began in 1992 by French computer scientist Christophe de Dinechin, and while it is influenced by C++ and Ada, programmers can extend it via their own plug-ins and develop their own syntax.

Different sub-teams are involved in tightly defining complex 3D games.

SOLVING PROBLEMS WITH CODE

SOLVING PROBLEMS WITH CODE
GLOSSARY

asymmetric encryption This is a form of secret message sharing in which the sender and recipient each have a secret key and a public key; messages are encoded using the public key and decrypted with the secret key.

control characters/non-printing characters The 33 non-printing characters in the original ASCII letter scheme common on early computers (inherited from teletype machines). They created compatibility issues as computer designers found different uses for them than they'd had in teletype machines (where one was to sound the bell).

cryptocurrency A currency that is based not on a central bank, such as sterling or dollars, but exists in the cloud. Bitcoin is the most famous example.

cryptography The art of turning messages into code (and attempting to break the code of others' messages).

DARPA The Defense Advanced Research Projects Agency (founded as ARPA in 1958) is tasked with making investments to improve technology that can be used to defend the USA. The internet is founded on ARPANET – a technology the agency created.

feature vector In machine learning software, a feature vector is a numerical representation of the value being analysed (as computers find it easier to process numbers).

for loop A repeated instruction, usually until a certain condition is met. The program keeps going over a certain section, perhaps adding one to the memory each time.

hardcode In programming, to hardcode something into a project is to code something you're unlikely to change (and, by extension, code in a way that will make it difficult for someone given that task later) – 'He hardcoded this in'.

HTML Hypertext Markup Language – the language for programming web pages, which uses codes such as <B> **to start bold and** </B> to end a bold section.

JPEG Acronym for Joint Photographic Experts Group, who designed the very popular JPEG file format, which is used for compressing photographic files by discarding some data. It is a lossy file format, and you can choose the level of loss when you create the file.

lossy In the context of file compression, 'lossy' means that some level of detail will be sacrificed to achieve a smaller file size (appropriate with images, video and audio but not text).

operator In an equation or algorithm, symbols such as + – that perform functions are 'operators'. The numbers or variables they affect are 'operands'.

PGP Pretty Good Privacy, an encryption system.

shear mapping The shear is a measure of the extent to which a vertical line leans from pointing straight up. Identifying a shear is useful in software functions such as facial detection because people can tilt their heads.

symmetrical encryption This is a form of secret message sharing in which both sender and recipient are using the same key.

terabyte 1024 gigabytes.

training data The information fed into a supervised machine learning system so it can develop the ability to make predictions on data it has no knowledge of.

vector On a computer, a vector file is a graphic described using geometry and maths rather than pixels, such as in a photograph. Many line drawings and logos are vectors as they are efficient in terms of file size, and can be scaled infinitely.

ZIP A popular compressed file format.

ALGORITHMS

the 30-second code

Computers will only do what we tell them to do, using the method we give them, carrying out each step in the order described by our code – we can't fly before we've reached the airport. We hear a lot about 'the algorithm' that controls what we see on social media, but the concept of algorithms originates with mathematics and predates computers. Computer programs are made up of algorithms, each of which gives the computer a set of steps to follow in order to obtain the desired outcome, as with a travel plan. For example, if we want to get from London to San Diego, there are a number of different ways we could do it. First we must reach Heathrow Airport via some form of transport. Then, flying direct is the most expensive method because of the monopoly on the route. We could transit in different US cities once or twice along the way, which costs us time as opposed to money. We could fly to Los Angeles or San Francisco and drive the rest of the way for the experience. The set of steps that precisely describes each London to San Diego journey forms an algorithm for taking our trip. One of the skills a programmer needs is to be able to select the best algorithm for a task.

RELATED TOPICS
See also
LOOPS & ITERATIONS
page 72

FUNCTIONS
page 76

DATABASE OPERATION: CRUD
page 92

3-SECOND BIOGRAPHY
MUHAMMAD IBN MUSA
AL-KHWARIZMI
c. 780–850
When Latinized in the 12th century, the work of this Persian mathematician was headed *Dixit Algorizmi* ('so said al-Khwarizmi'), from which we derive the words 'arithmetic' and 'algorithm'

30-SECOND TEXT
Suze Shardlow

3-SECOND BIT
Algorithms are precise instructions; to create an algorithm in code is to define a task for computers to achieve (though there might be more than one solution to a problem).

3-MINUTE BYTE
Sorting, searching and matching are three of the most common things we ask a computer to do. We might want to sort itineraries by travel time and price or filter the ones that transit in Los Angeles. For each of those tasks, there are different algorithms we could use. For example, we use a different method for sorting flight lengths than we do to sort airline names.

Algorithms form tasks for computers to achieve desired outcomes, such as flight plans.

THE FIZZBUZZ TEST
the 30-second code

A new programmer can expect to encounter a raft of problems, some for work and others to test their abilities. Tech blogger Imran Ghory promoted one of the most famous problems, FizzBuzz, as an interview test for coders. Fizz Buzz is a game children play (probably in maths lessons); the rules are simply to count up, one at a time, but to substitute the word 'Fizz' if the number is divisible by three, 'Buzz' if divisible by five and' Fizz Buzz' if divisible by both. Ghory was mostly interested in speed, but because the test can be solved a number of ways in code it also offers an insight into a problem-solving approach. For example, do you hardcode the numbers 3 and 5 into the code, or ask for inputs? Could there be more than two substitute words? Oh, and how far do you want to go? You could produce answers until the user escapes the program, but it is more elegant to create a loop, so you might choose to ask the user how far to play the game, or just hardcode in a number like 50? An interviewer might even be interested to see what you call the variable of that for loop – i (for iteration) is traditional.

3-SECOND BIT
Fizz Buzz is the game your parents or maths teachers use to promote quick mental arithmetic and has also become a classic test of aspiring programmers.

3-MINUTE BYTE
Assessing whether a number is divisible by something in software is achieved using what is called a modulo operator. To see if i is divisible by 3, you would check if ($i\%3==0$), which, broken down, is whether the remainder of i divided by 3 is not equal to 0. So if i was 31 the modulo would be 0.333, which isn't zero.

RELATED TOPICS
See also
LOOPS & ITERATIONS
page 72

3-SECOND BIOGRAPHIES
JEFF ATWOOD
1970–
American software developer and co-founder of Stack Overflow, where Ghory's FizzBuzz idea caught a wider audience

IMRAN GHORY
1982–
Computer science graduate responsible for the Theory of Geek cartoon and SeedTable, an early census of start-ups

30-SECOND TEXT
Mark Steadman

Fizz Buzz is a maths game children play, but is a classic interview test for coders.

```javascript
function isMultiple (num, mod) {
  return num % mod === 0;
}

function main() {

  let output = "";

  for (let i = 1; i <= 100; i++) {

    switch (true) {

      case isMultiple(i, 15):
        output = "FizzBuzz";
        break;

      case isMultip    3):
        output = "Fi
        break;

      cas
        ou
      , break;

      default
        o

    }

    console.log    tpu
  }

}
```

SORTING & BIG O NOTATION

the 30-second code

If we had an array of cats and kittens, how would we sort them into ascending order of size? If it's a small enough group of cats, we could probably eyeball the felines and quickly pick out the smallest to largest. How does a computer do it? It can't look at the whole group like we do: it needs to move through them systematically and look at the cats one by one. However, there are many different sorting algorithms. One of these is the bubble sort, which sees the computer moving through the array and switching pairs so the larger cat is on the right. This can take a number of passes before the sort is complete. Big O notation is how we express an algorithm's efficiency in terms of how much longer it takes and how much more space it uses as you increase the size of the input data set. Programmers need to know this so they can select the best algorithm for the task, especially when working on large-scale applications. An efficient algorithm would be O(1) – a result in one operation like 'print last item on list'. If you think of banking software that handles millions of transactions per day, small inefficiencies in the code can add up to huge costs in time and therefore money.

3-SECOND BIT
To work out how efficient a sorting algorithm is, you compare the number of computing operations (O) versus the total number (n) of items of data being sorted.

3-MINUTE BYTE
Different sort algorithms use different methods. Contrast bubble sort with merge sort, which splits the cats into smaller groups, sorts each group separately, then merges them. Each operation takes time. Splitting cats would be one operation, each comparison counts as one, then moving a cat counts as one. Big O notation describes an algorithm's relative efficiency by defining how the number of steps required changes as the data set grows.

RELATED TOPICS
See also
DATA TYPES
page 62

DATA STRUCTURES: ARRAYS
page 66

3-SECOND BIOGRAPHIES
PAUL GUSTAV HEINRICH BACHMANN
1837–1920
German mathematician who created five volumes on number theory and is credited, with Edmund Landau, for Big O notation

DONALD KNUTH
1938–
American computer scientist, Turing Award winner and author of the multi-volume *The Art of Computer Programming*, popularizing the use of Big O notation to assess the efficiency of an algorithm

30-SECOND TEXT
Suze Shardlow

Sort algorithms sort items of data, such as the cats in an array of different sizes.

THE TWO GENERALS PROBLEM

the 30-second code

3-SECOND BIT
The similarities between computer-to-computer communication and medieval military runners in one problem.

3-MINUTE BYTE
One of the most famous failures of the two generals problem happened to British takeaway delivery service Deliveroo in September 2018, when the system failed to acknowledge numerous orders (even though it had accepted them). In turn, many customers re-sent identical orders. Some ended up with lots of food, all were charged for each order and Deliveroo had a lot apologizing to do.

This classic theoretical paradox is used to teach networking. Like all good hypotheticals, it can't be solved by getting the generals better equipment. The problem is this: there is a heavily armoured castle at the bottom of a valley and at the top of the valley are two armies – each led by a general – amassed on opposite sides. To conquer the castle they must charge at exactly the same time, but they need to communicate via messenger to agree a time and they can't be 100 per cent sure that the messenger has survived the trip. The first general needs to know their message is received and understood by the second general before attacking. You might think the solution is a second messenger bringing a copy of the message back with a receipt, but, of course, that second messenger is just as likely to succumb to hostile fire as they cross the valley. In fact there is no theoretical solution. A pragmatic solution is an idempotency token – a unique value added to the message (cart ID) by the sending general (or app, or server), which is logged at the sending and receiving end. People generally re-send failed orders/messages, but if it has the same token, the receiving server (General B) can ignore it knowing that it has dealt with the order already.

RELATED TOPICS
See also
EVENTUAL CONSISTENCY
page 82

THE FIZZBUZZ TEST
page 114

3-SECOND BIOGRAPHY
JIM GRAY
1944–2012
American computer scientist and Turing Award winner, credited not with the proof of the two generals problem but naming it and making it famous in 1978. His sailboat disappeared in 2007 and he was declared legally dead in 2012

30-SECOND TEXT
Adam Juniper

The two generals problem is a thought experiment to show the issues encountered by an unreliable link.

COMPRESSION & THE HUFFMAN TREE

the 30-second code

Computers work with a finite amount of data storage and the internet has limited bandwidth, so reducing file sizes is useful. Huffman coding is a method named for its creator. Invented in 1952, it handles text compression with what's known as a 'lossless' approach (as opposed to 'lossy' compression, which sacrifices detail, such as JPEGs or most video compression). At their most basic level, computers handle a stream of 1s and 0s, and text (at least when Huffman was working) used one byte (eight bits) for each character – for example, lower case a is 01100001. This was enough for the basic English alphabet and punctuation (all that mattered to the early computer engineers), but still quickly searchable at machine level. Huffman's innovation was that any large text document could be examined by the computer to create a 'Huffman Tree'. This was a key telling the computer which letter to add as it decompressed the file in sequence. This sacrificed speed, but made it possible to assign fewer bits than a whole byte to more frequently used characters. Because tree branches end at letters, decompression could confidently place a letter regardless of the number of bits. In the years since, lossless compression such as ZIP has come along, which improves efficiency by compressing more than one byte at a time.

RELATED TOPICS

See also
BINARY & BITS
page 60

UNICODE
page 126

3-SECOND BIOGRAPHY
DAVID A. HUFFMAN
1925–99
American electrical engineer who, after Huffman coding, was a pioneer of mathematical origami

30-SECOND TEXT
Adam Juniper

3-SECOND BIT
Storing data as efficiently as possibly is called compression, and it might sacrifice speed but will save on drive space and bandwidth costs.

3-MINUTE BYTE
Lossy compression enables images and video to be transmitted digitally and it works by discarding detail that the eye won't notice. A single frame of 4K video (assuming it wasn't HDR) would use 4096*2160*24 = 26,542,080 bits, or 25.3Mb. That makes a 90-minute feature film over 3 terabytes. Video compression algorithms not only trim detail, but only send some frames (keyframes) and then describe only the differences.

Huffman coding is a method of compressing files to store data as efficiently as possible.

SEARCH ENGINE OPTIMIZATION

the 30-second code

3-SECOND BIT
Search engines use computers to read and rank internet pages, so content creators (and their coders) will always need to appeal to machines as well as people.

3-MINUTE BYTE
SEO is divided into two elements, on-page and off-page. The former means making the individual page itself more appealing to the engine, including using the right tags to highlight keywords and ensuring the server delivers the page quickly. Off-page SEO is the process of link-building – getting a page to appear in as many places as possible. This may involve a lot of social media work, such as reaching out to blogs and similar sites.

As already mentioned, coding online doesn't just include traditional 'programming'; the content itself is embedded into what is essentially a programming language: HTML. That creates the opportunity not only for readers to browse pages, but for machines to examine the text of a page to identify the most important words (keywords). HTML tags (the code) actually help with this because they identify the headlines or pieces that should be in bold. Google's original innovation was to write code that 'read' through pages on the internet, building a database of the important content. It was able to find the address of pages to look for by 'crawling' – that is, to use the link tags and follow them for the next page to index, and so on. The more links Google found to any one page, the more important it thought it was, and the higher it ranked it. Google's ranking, in turn, is the beginning of a whole new industry: search engine optimization (SEO), which means making your content more appealing to, well, Google, who dominate the search market. SEO as an industry includes attempting to decipher the (ever-changing) algorithm used by Google to identify and rank pages, then appeal to it, be that in the use of code, structure or content.

RELATED TOPICS
See also
WEB DEVELOPMENT
page 94

ALGORITHMS
page 112

LARRY PAGE
page 132

3-SECOND BIOGRAPHY
SERGEY BRIN
1973–
Russian-born co-founder of Google, met Larry Page at Stanford and used his interest in data mining to co-write the predecessor to Google, BackRub, in 1996

30-SECOND TEXT
Adam Juniper

SEO attempts to look at the algorithms hidden in search engines to better target specific users.

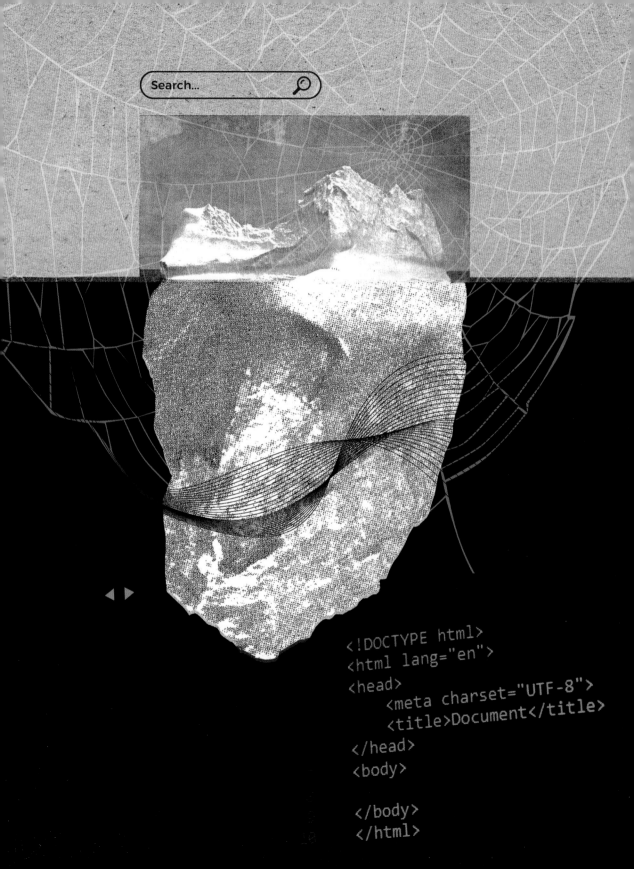

FACE DETECTION

the 30-second code

Humans are incredibly adept at recognizing faces (even if we can't always remember the associated name). This has clear evolutionary advantages for a social creature, and a study at the University of Louvain, Belgium, used fMRI scanners to identify the fusiform gyrus – the part of the brain that distinguishes faces. Scientists have also seen that humans seem to work by identifying first that they're looking at a face (detection), before going on to work out if they recognize the individual and how they're feeling. When Facebook began large-scale facial recognition in 2010, it started the same way. Recognition works through comparison, for which computers need data (other pictures of faces). To work at speed, the computer also needs to compare as few numbers as possible, so a grid (feature vector) is built of key features, and the proportions between them can be measured. The face may not face the camera directly (a shear), but the measurements of the ratios are enough. More recently, facial recognition has grown and offshoots include specific development based on low-quality images (such as those from security cameras) and 3D facial recognition. Apple's Face ID projects over 30,000 infrared dots towards the user's face to create a contour map of it (used for ID and photographic effects such as blurred backgrounds).

3-SECOND BIT
Identifying and detecting faces (and objects) – computer vision – are common tasks in computing, and very complex, but for programmers it's all about libraries and databases.

3-MINUTE BYTE
Computer scientists began work on facial recognition in the 1960s, manually identifying the coordinates of features with a graphics tablet. There have been advances at DARPA and elsewhere, but now a programmer looking to incorporate facial recognition into their project would turn to one of the code libraries, such as Open CV, which has grown from a project Intel began in 1999.

RELATED TOPICS
See also
ALGORITHMS
page 112

AI: ARTIFICIAL INTELLIGENCE
page 138

3-SECOND BIOGRAPHY
WOODROW WILSON BLEDSOE
1921–95
American mathematician and computer scientist, 'Woody' Bledsoe was a founder of AI technology and wrote a paper on pattern recognition as early as 1959

30-SECOND TEXT
Adam Juniper

Grids are built of key features to allow computers to detect faces at speed.

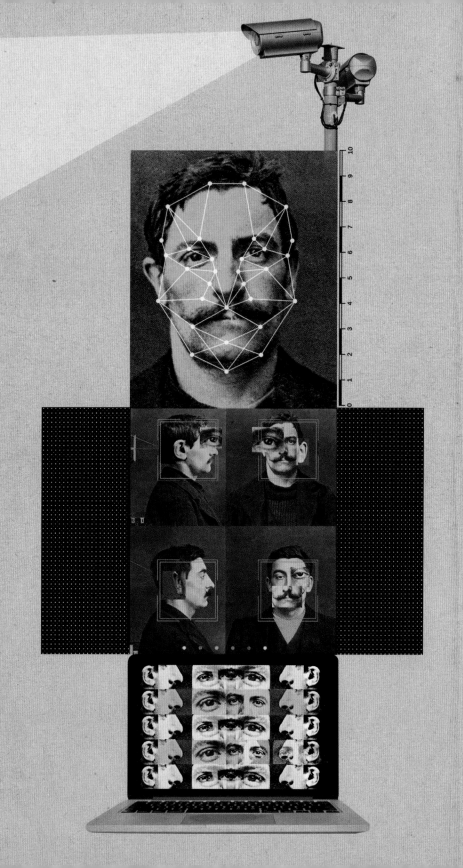

UNICODE

the 30-second code

In the era of teletype, a straightforward code to translate English to binary for telegrams was needed, and the solution was the 'American Standard Code for Information Interchange' (ASCII), created in 1960. As a 7-bit format, it has 128 characters: 0–9, A–Z, a–z, punctuation and 33 non-printing characters (we still use 0001101, carriage return and tab, but not 'bell' so much). This was all very well for English-language telegrams, but computer designers found different uses for those control characters, leading to one ASCII text file behaving differently across operating systems. To compound the issue, many chose to add an eighth bit to the character codes (8-bit, 256 possible characters), creating various 'Extended ASCII' sets to suit local language needs. In 1988 Joe Becker proposed a new 16-bit system, simply adding nine 'off' bits to the beginning of old ASCII characters so 1110100 (t), would be 0000000001110100 in a Unicode file, an easy translation, but there would be 65,536 characters available, enough to support every language on Earth. Four years later the Unicode Consortium was incorporated, and had converts around the world at leading firms, including Apple. For a while, it appeared that was it – then emoji happened, and the consortium also took on the related role of defining the symbols.

RELATED TOPICS
See also
INSTRUCTION SETS & STORED PROGRAMS
page 28

DATA STRUCTURES: ARRAYS
page 66

3-SECOND BIOGRAPHIES
JOE BECKER
1948–
American computer scientist, the 'father of Unicode', Becker worked at Xerox's famed Palo Alto R&D

MARK CRISPIN
1956–2012
American systems programmer, creator of IMAP email and helped build the Unicode standard

30-SECOND TEXT
Adam Juniper

3-SECOND BIT
A global standard for text and emoji.

3-MINUTE BYTE
The Unicode Consortium is responsible for maintaining which underlying binary code in a digital file (or web page) translates as which character on screen. That includes not just the symbols we recognize as language, but emoji too. Fonts might have a different letter 'a' (or a different looking 'smiley'), but the fact is an 'a' or a 'smiley' derives from Unicode.

Unicode is the global standard for text and emoji.

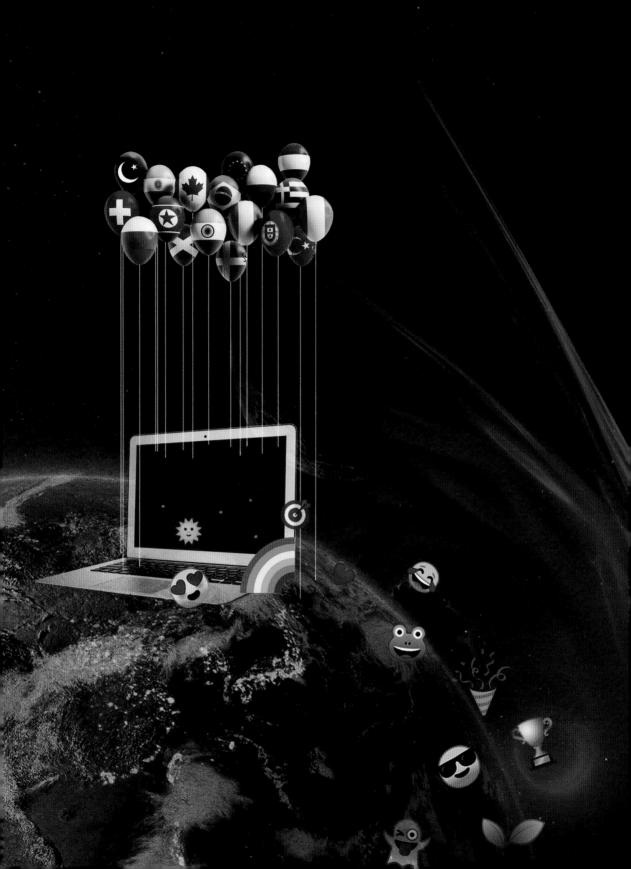

END-TO-END ENCRYPTION

the 30-second code

Traditional cryptography involves protecting messages using a single, private key – known as symmetric encryption. If Alice wished to send Bob a private message, she would encrypt it using the private key and send it. No one who intercepted it could understand it, but Bob would be able to use the key to decrypt it. The problem with this approach online is how Alice gives Bob that key in the first place – the message is travelling online, and the object of the encryption is to prevent hackers gaining access to the message. The solution is public-key encryption. Alice and Bob both need public and private keys. Alice can look at Bob's public key and use that to encrypt the message. She can then send it, but only the private key can be used to decrypt it, and only Bob has a copy of his own private key. RSA, one of the first public-key cryptosystems, achieves this using prime numbers, which are easier to calculate one way but not the other. Secure HTTP, Pretty Good Privacy (PGP) and cryptocurrencies use this approach. Beyond this is the Diffie-Hellman method of secret key exchange, known as asymmetric encryption, in which Alice and Bob can generate a shared secret key by combining their own keys with a public key (a prime).

RELATED TOPICS
See also
WHAT IS BLOCKCHAIN?
page 144

3-SECOND BIT
Sending data, from photos to credit card numbers, depends on being able to encrypt information without first getting together and planning a code. This is how it's done.

3-MINUTE BYTE
Politicians occasionally describe end-to-end encryption as a threat to society as it prevents government agencies getting legally approved access (like traditional wiretaps). Online, however, obscuring the message from the routers and servers carrying it means that the message (or image) isn't in readable form at any point on its journey (when a hacker or disgruntled social media employee might view it). A backdoor might sound useful for the police, but can be found by bad actors too.

3-SECOND BIOGRAPHIES
LEONARD ADLEMAN
1945–
American computer scientist who received the Turing Award in 2000 for co-creating RSA encryption, which he publicly described in 1977

CLIFFORD COCKS
1950–
British cryptographer who actually co-invented public key encryption in 1973 while working at GCHQ, but couldn't reveal it for 30 years

30-SECOND TEXT
Adam Juniper

Alice and Bob sending each other encrypted messages.

PATTERN MATCHING LANGUAGES

the 30-second code

3-SECOND BIT
Pattern matching languages exist as a way of helping academics query data using the strict logic of a computer.

3-MINUTE BYTE
Pattern matching is not the same thing as pattern recognition. The former is based on absolutes, while the latter (like facial recognition) is based on identifying similarities. It is something humans have little trouble achieving and computers were not traditionally suited to, but machine learning can. Pattern recognition can include speech recognition, document recognition, facial recognition and medical diagnosis, and is usually achieved by building vectors from training data.

There are many who are trained in one or another programming language and end up with the simple impression that first there were procedural languages, and following that there was object-orientated programming (OOP) and that is the extent of the progression. In fact, there are more programming paradigms; functions may or may not be considered objects, for a start, but an entirely different approach is a pattern matching language such as Prolog, first developed in the 1970s. This uses the language's grammar to describe all the constraints of an environment or data set in clear terms – variables, constants and facts – much like a formal logic question from a philosophy paper. The data is effectively being added into the system together with its constraints in order. The actual pattern matching happens when you query the system; inside it tests the variables based on the facts and attempts to indicate what is 'true'. This also makes Prolog well suited to solving algebraic questions; queries are structured: `?- mother (X, arya).` (Who is Arya's mother?). Assuming all the data is there, that returns 'Catelyn'. There's more to this than meets the eye though – if Catelyn was defined as one of several parents, then the declarations would also need to list Catelyn as female.

RELATED TOPICS
See also
FORTRAN: THE FIRST
HIGH-LEVEL LANGUAGE
page 42

PROCEDURAL LANGUAGES
page 46

COMPILED CODE
page 48

OBJECT-ORIENTED
PROGRAMMING (OOP)
page 50

3-SECOND BIOGRAPHY
ALAIN COLMERAUER
1941–2017
French computer scientist who worked on early translation systems and created logic language Prolog

30-SECOND TEXT
Adam Juniper

By using the strict logic of a computer, academics use pattern matching in order to help them query data.

26 March 1973
Born Lawrence Edward Page in Lansing, Michigan, USA

1990
Attends the high-profile Interlochen Center for the Arts music camp for two summers, playing flute

1996
With limited HTML, sets up a very plain-looking search page for his nascent search engine

1998
Founds the company Google with Sergey Brin

2000
Google announces in a press release that it has indexed 1 billion URLs (web addresses)

2001
Page steps down as CEO of Google in response to pressure from prominent Silicon Valley investors who sought a leader with more business experience before providing $50 million

2004
Google makes its Initial Public Offering (IPO), making Page a billionaire

2005
Page acquires the Android platform for $50 million without checking with Google CEO Eric Schmidt (by this point $50 million wasn't a big sum for Google)

2007
Marries scientist Lucinda Southworth on Richard Branson's private island

2011
Page re-assumes the role of CEO at Google, now a company with $180 billion market cap. He tweets: 'Adult supervision no longer needed'

2013
Addressing the Google I/O developers' conference in San Francisco, says in his keynote address that: 'We're at maybe 1 per cent of what is possible … we should be focusing on the things that don't exist'

2015
Becomes CEO of Alphabet, a new holding company to contain Google and other companies

2019
Steps down as CEO of Alphabet (Google's holding company)

LARRY PAGE

Larry Page was born into a computing family; his father was a pioneer in computer science and AI and his mother taught programming at Michigan State University. His childhood home was littered with technology (he was the first child in his elementary school to use a word processor for an assignment). He was an avid reader who saw Nikola Tesla as an idol, and also found time to play instruments and compose music. He has connected that love of music with an understanding of timing and speed in computing.

Page studied at Michigan University, where he helped build a solar car for a competition, drafted a business plan for a software-based music synthesizer and even suggested the campus should have a driverless monorail. He went on to Stanford, where he would gain a master's degree in computer science and enrol on the PhD programme. With the guidance of supervisor Terry Winograd, he chose to explore the maths of the World Wide Web as a research topic.

Working on the problem of analysing links in web pages, he was soon joined by fellow student Sergey Brin. Until then, Brin had not found a project that engaged his interest like Page's problem. Their project was nicknamed 'BackRub' (a pun on the 'backlinks' in web pages), though their research paper was called 'The Anatomy of a Large-Scale Hypertextual Web Search Engine'. BackRub already needed more computing power to examine the 10 million pages of the Web (in 1996) than they had access to as students, so they began connecting more machines. Page's dorm room became a machine lab connected to the university's internet network, using a Sun Ultra series II with a 28GB disk for its main database and a few other machines to handle the load of building the database and handling searches. It was coded in Java and Python.

After the creation of a public search page, the site began to grow, reaching 10,000 searches a day by mid-1998, at which point the pair began to solicit funds and incorporated the company, initially choosing the name Googol (this literally means 10 to the power of 100), but reputedly went with an accidental misspelling.

The company then moved to Silicon Valley and began to grow a more traditional management structure – something Page was initially sceptical of but after meeting with other tech CEOs, including Steve Jobs, accepted. Others have, nevertheless, described the period he was not CEO as Google's 'lost decade', though the growth suggests otherwise.

From the mid-2010s, Page has been increasingly known for his other interests, including philanthropic projects and even flying cars. He has steadily backed away from day-to-day decision-making at Google.

Adam Juniper

MODERN CONCERNS & CONCEPTS

MODERN CONCERNS & CONCEPTS
GLOSSARY

artificial neural network A system made of successive layers of nodes – artificial neurons – that has similarities to the structure of an animal brain.

boot camp A popular phrase among programmers for initial training in a language or skill (even though very few of them will have attended military training).

build The process of converting a program as code into a program that can be executed (run), for example, 'There were six builds before we had one that worked'.

challenge test A test that challenges the user to perform a task, for example a CAPTCHA, in which you need to choose which of 16 photos have bikes in.

crawler A piece of software that 'visits' websites to collect data; Google's crawler, for example, builds up its knowledge of the internet this way.

cryptocurrency A currency backed by an online digital ledger rather than traditional printed notes tied to a national bank.

headless browsers Programs, such as PhantomJS and CasperJS, that can be told to 'visit' websites and collect information or test aspects of them, but are also often abused by hackers.

layer Artificial neurons typically take inputs as a set, then pass their results on to the next set – these sets are called 'layers' (or hidden layers) and there may be several between the input and decision of the system.

machine learning Automated data analysis/ pattern identification that forms a branch of artificial intelligence.

Nutch Early headless browser.

public-key cryptopgraphy An effective means of hiding data being sent from one user to another without first having to send a private key, invented in the 1970s and the fundamental basis of most internet security.

'the algorithm' When a major web application's systems are not fully understood, they are often referred to as 'the algorithm', especially by users who are affected by the results.

training data The information fed into a supervised machine learning system so it can develop the ability to make predictions on data it has no knowledge of.

version control system A means of monitoring who is developing software and keeping it up to date.

AI: ARTIFICIAL INTELLIGENCE

the 30-second code

For centuries, humans have been seeking ways to make tasks faster, more efficient and less strenuous. Much of our production and manufacturing is now carried out by machines that are sometimes operated by humans and often controlled by computers. Artificial intelligence (AI) is the area of computing that takes coding beyond just telling the machine what to do and into the realm of creating programs that think like humans. The computer can then plan, make decisions and solve problems for us, for example, when we use our smartphone to plan a journey based on parameters we give it. We may make a wrong turn, so the software has to recalculate the route. AI is part of our daily lives; it gathers data on our previous actions and habits to give us what it thinks we need, want or what we might spend money on. What we often think of as 'the algorithm' is actually AI, for example, the posts and advertisements we see on social media. It's also being used to advance other areas of science, such as healthcare, to help physicians manage, cure and prevent medical conditions. There is always still an element of human intervention as AI is not yet perfect, but neither is human decision-making.

RELATED TOPICS
See also
FACE DETECTION
page 124

COMPUTERS CANNOT
DETERMINE TRUTH
page 142

3-SECOND BIOGRAPHY
LARRY TESLER
1945–2020
American computer scientist who worked at Xerox PARC, Apple, Amazon and Yahoo, noted for making cut and paste so simple, helping ARM processors spread so widely and his so-called theorem: 'AI is whatever hasn't been done yet.'

30-SECOND TEXT
Suze Shardlow

3-SECOND BIT
AI systems are trained to solve human problems by feeding them data (at the risk of privacy).

3-MINUTE BYTE
Artificial intelligence is an umbrella concept that includes machine learning. AI systems are trained to solve problems by feeding them data: example situations and desired outcomes. The AI's algorithms build a model from this data. A sufficiently trained AI system can use its model to infer likely outcomes for new situations that weren't part of the training data, for example smartphones and predictive text. This process mimics the human learning experience.

AI systems are made to think like humans in order for them to solve problems for us.

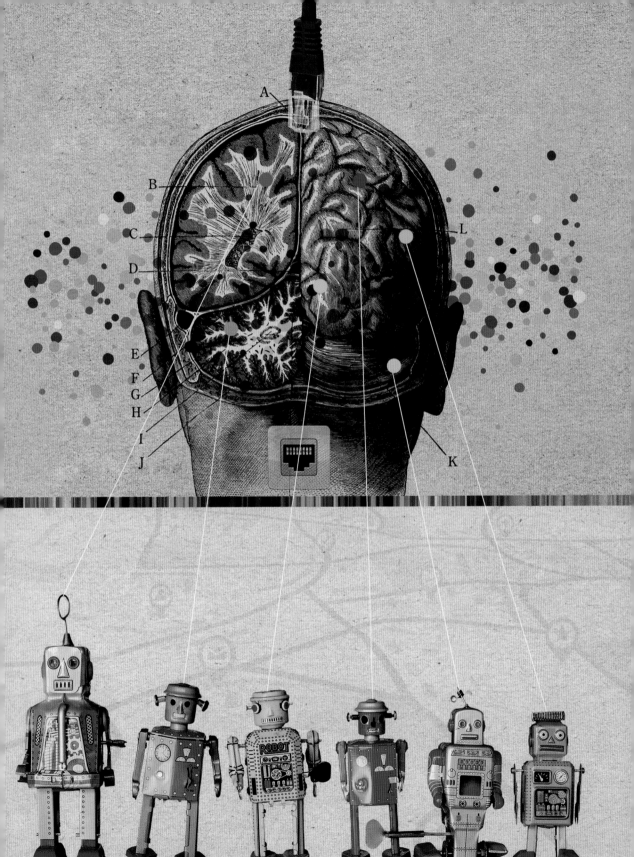

BLACK BOX

the 30-second code

3-SECOND BIT
Black boxes are hidden to the user (even where that user is a programmer or tester), and can contain a simple function or an artificial neural network.

3-MINUTE BYTE
One of the most famous examples of a black box, in this sense, is what web developers or social media creators call 'the algorithm' but is, in practice, a collection of numerous AI systems that work together to rank pages or identify content to censor. Content creators who engage in search engine optimization (SEO), or otherwise optimizing their content, are essentially engaging in black-box testing.

In computer science, a black box is anything you can test without knowing how it works. You send an input, the black box does its job and you check to see if it gives you the output you expected. Indeed, many library functions are effectively black boxes to the programmers who use them. When it comes to testing, the black-box approach can be seen as user-centric, and means you can use testers who have no experience of programming or the software's structure. Black-box methods include boundary value analysis (testing values just inside and outside those that should work), equivalence partitioning (picking representative inputs) and cause–effect graphing. In recent years, the metaphorical black box has started to present a broader issue – humans now trust their safety to AI-based systems that make more complex decisions from given inputs than we can feasibly assess. We don't even know what the 'expected' result is. The 'neural net', which is the basis of a lot of AI, is made up of a layered hierarchy of binary tests that computer scientists call nodes but, like neurons, they light up or don't. Machine learning begins with a testing phase, and automatically re-structures its nodes until they are generating the right result. French computer scientist Yann LeCun called it 'a box with millions of knobs'.

RELATED TOPICS
See also
DEBUGGING
page 104

AI: ARTIFICIAL INTELLIGENCE
page 138

3-SECOND BIOGRAPHY
WARREN MCCULLOCH
1898–1969
American neurophysiologist who, with Walter Pitts, first created a computational model for the neural network

30-SECOND TEXT
Adam Juniper

Black boxes are hidden to the user and tests if an input outputs in the expected way.

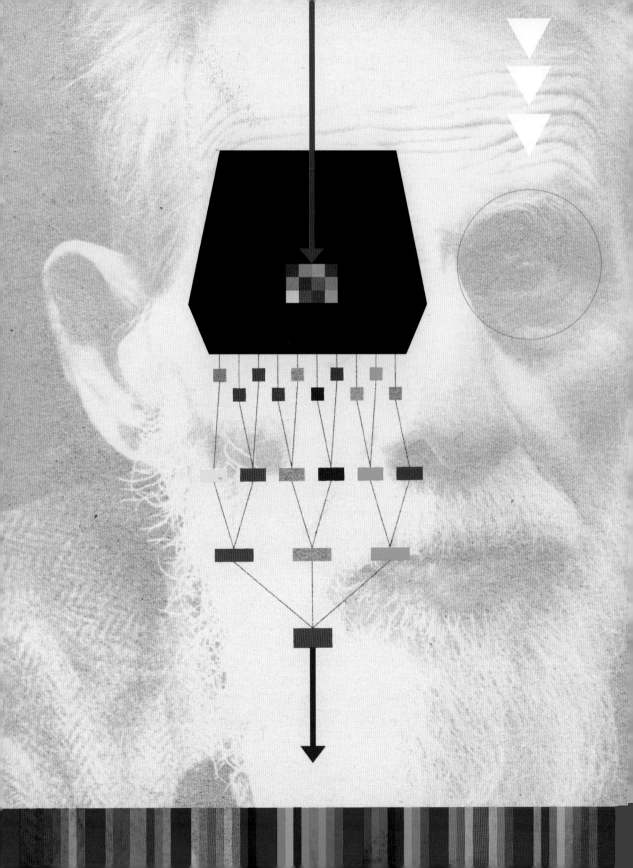

COMPUTERS CANNOT DETERMINE TRUTH

the 30-second code

There have been numerous attempts to determine objective truth using technology; fans of US cop shows will be familiar with the polygraph (lie detector), for example. This is an analogue technology, tracking blood pressure, pulse, breathing and sweat, with the idea that patterns in these measurements reveal a lie. (It has been shown to be fundamentally flawed and unreliable, relying on a belief in guilt and shame, but is also a $2 billion industry in the US alone.) Demand has grown for a digital equivalent for truth in the media. This stems from an issue in 'the algorithm' of YouTube and others, which look to identify and share 'authoritative voices' that also meet the criteria for garnering more views and keeping people looking at the host's advertisers. As tabloid newspapers showed for years, inciting fear and shock drew more sales (or clicks) than carefully citing respected sources. Since authority and views are connected, the system can easily determine authority from views, and award more views to more shocking content. How, then, can a platform detect and ban a lie without breaking freedom of speech or making itself so dull no one visits in the first place? One route is to start with a policy and a human enforcement team.

3-SECOND BIT
While humanity is aware of the risks, as well as the virtues, of near-unlimited free speech, software seems unlikely to find a solution.

3-MINUTE BYTE
In 2020, Twitter's fact-checking label put it in then-president Trump's firing line. Twitter's method was to create a set of rules, then to add warnings to tweets that seemed to break them, or directions to facts from trusted sources (implying that POTUS wasn't one of them). The company uses 'internal systems' (algorithmic) quotes from 'trusted partners' (for example, NBC). Cleverly it puts these partners' fact-checks on a Twitter page, where it can still sell advertising space.

RELATED TOPICS
See also
AI: ARTIFICIAL INTELLIGENCE
page 138

DETECTING BOTS
page 146

3-SECOND BIOGRAPHY
CHARLES GOODHART
1936–
British economist who said: 'When a metric becomes a target, it ceases to be a good measure.' In the context of fact-checking, it suggests people will be trying to find ways to become 'trusted'

30-SECOND TEXT
Adam Juniper

Despite numerous attempts, technology is still flawed when trying to detect false information.

WHAT IS BLOCKCHAIN?

the 30-second code

3-SECOND BIT
A technology to replace cash and other sequential transactions that can be deployed as a public system (like Bitcoin) or within a corporation.

3-MINUTE BYTE
A blockchain could be controlled on a single server, but instead you, Alice and Bob can all keep a copy (and keep it updated). If I decide to give Bob 40 coin, I broadcast that block to the whole network of coin users. Everyone needs to be sure the blockchain is in the correct order, and testing that requires computational work; Bitcoin rewards this with new currency, so it is known as mining.

Blockchain is the underlying technology behind Bitcoin and the many other digital currencies that have emerged in recent years. It works by creating a digital ledger of transactions between users, which are secured using public-key cryptography. It is a separate trusted environment that isn't directly tied to any traditional currency. If you regularly exchanged money with Alice and Bob, you could set up a cryptocurrency. Let's say you all put £100 each in the pot and gave yourself 100 coin each, then Alice wants to pay you 50 coin, she would create the first transaction: '1: Alice Pays You 50' followed by Alice's digital signature. Now Bob pays you 40 coin; the transaction on the ledger is '2: Bob Pays You 40' followed by Bob's digital signature. Now, if Alice were to decide to buy a hat from Bob for 70 coin, she couldn't, as the ledger says she only has 50. The sequencing numbers on the transactions are important for two reasons: it is crucial to the cryptography, but it also forms the chain. Each transaction is a block, they happen in a specific order, and that is how we can be sure Alice only has 50 coin after the first two transactions.

RELATED TOPICS
See also
EVENTUAL CONSISTENCY
page 82

END-TO-END ENCRYPTION
page 128

3-SECOND BIOGRAPHY
SATOSHI NAKAMOTO
1975– (claimed)
This is the pseudonym for the inventor(s) of Bitcoin; you'll see the name and speculation about it all over the Web

30-SECOND TEXT
Adam Juniper

Digital currencies such as Bitcoin are built of blockchain technology.

DETECTING BOTS

the 30-second code

RELATED TOPICS
See also
END-TO-END ENCRYPTION
page 128

AI: ARTIFICIAL INTELLIGENCE
page 138

ALAN TURING
page 150

3-SECOND BIT
Bots are pieces of code that attempt to access your program or site, and they are ever more sophisticated at pretending to be humans.

3-MINUTE BYTE
One method of bot detection that was prevalent from 2009 was Google's ReCAPTCHA, though you might not know that is a Google copyright but an acronym for 'Completely Automated Public Turing test to tell Computers and Humans Apart'. This is known as a Challenge-Response method – the server challenges the visitor in a way computers struggle with and you must respond. (PayPal began using a CAPTCHA in 2001.)

Bot, short for robot, is any code pretending to be human. This includes bad actors who write programs to hack secure systems. A very simple bot might be a program that repeatedly tries a password until it gets in (it'll also have to make a guess, perhaps from a list of popular passwords, before it tries them). A simple solution – which you've no doubt encountered – is for the protected system to only allow a few guesses before temporarily locking access to the account. When designing a program, you will need to consider how to approach detecting attempted hacks. Your approach will be different depending on whether it is a closed system (like the password on your computer) or one online. Up to a third of online traffic is bots attempting to crack protection, and they have evolved through several stages. The first bots were 'crawlers', which examined pages much like Google, but didn't maintain a cookie like a human visitor did. Next came web crawlers/headless browsers such as Nutch, which still looked different to real visitors, but the next generation – PhantomJS and CasperJS – is when the industry hit back with the challenge tests. JavaScript-based sites are even able to track mouse movements (as they build mountains of data for advertisers), which has led to bots that even attempt to mimic human mouse movements.

3-SECOND BIOGRAPHY
LUIS VON AHN
1978–
Guatemalan-American cryptography researcher who moved to CAPTCHA in 2000 and made the term famous in mainstream interviews

30-SECOND TEXT
Adam Juniper

Bots are pieces of code that try to access programs or sites by pretending to be human.

INTEGRATED DEVELOPMENT ENVIRONMENT

the 30-second code

Chapter 2 covered a lot of the

theory underlying modern object-orientated programming, but one thing that will be significant is where you do your programming. Just as there are word processors for writing, there are integrated development environments for programming, such as Apple's Xcode and Microsoft Visual Studio (available for Windows and Mac), though there are many more. These programs all have different features but the principal features are broadly the same. The main area (the equivalent of the area you type in a word processor) is an editor. This is the area for writing new programs; code is plain text, but typically the editor will highlight different elements to make the code easier to read (defined objects, functions, variables and so on). This is also helpful in boot camp and debugging as elements have to be spelt correctly to be highlighted! There is also an output or console area right next to the code area where the environment can run your code as you work, making it easier to debug (error warnings or incorrect calculations will appear here without the need to actually run a test). Finally, in a world of large teams, there might well be a connection to a shared team space or version control system, or a local library of your functions.

RELATED TOPICS

See also

PROCEDURAL LANGUAGES
page 46

COMPILED CODE
page 48

OBJECT ORIENTED
PROGRAMMING (OOP)
page 50

3-SECOND BIOGRAPHY
JOHN G. KEMENY
1926–92
Hungarian-born computer scientist behind Dartmouth BASIC, the first language designed to be programmed at a computer rather than on punch cards

30-SECOND TEXT
Adam Juniper

3-SECOND BIT
A nice thing about programming is that the people who do it know exactly how to write software to improve the experience.

3-MINUTE BYTE
The editor area might also be used to design application interfaces and connect pieces of code to particular elements. In XCode, for example, you can create a page for an iPhone app and add a button where you want it, and a type area on the same page. You can then write code that detects a press of the button, and changes the value being sent to the type area. You can even test it all on screen or send it to a test phone.

An editor can be used to design application interfaces and connect pieces of code to particular elements.

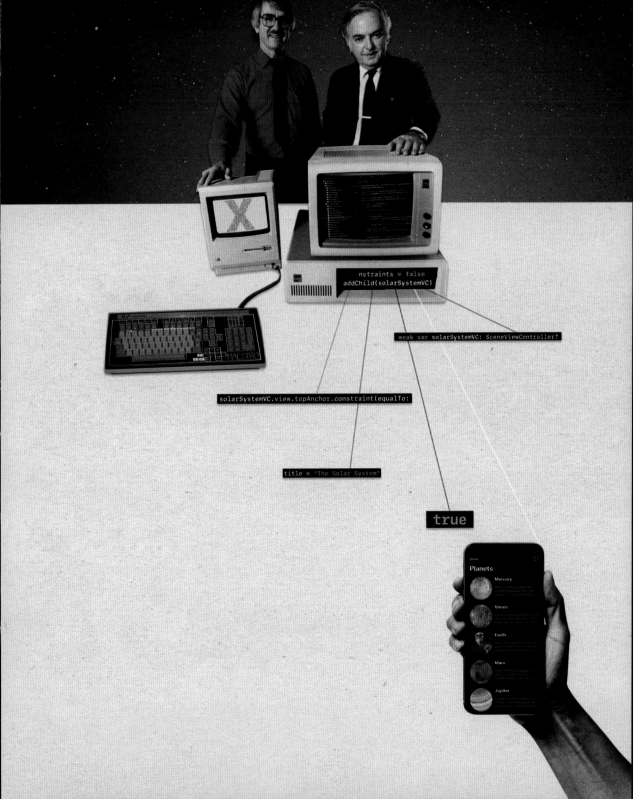

1912
Born in Maida Vale,
London

1926
Goes to a high-tier
boarding school, where
he meets Christopher
Morcom, his 'first love',
who dies of tuberculosis
in 1930

1931–34
Studies as an
undergraduate at King's
College, Cambridge

1935
Made a fellow of King's
College

1936
Publishes his paper 'On
Computable Numbers'
including the 'universal
machine' idea

1936–38
Studies under Alonzo
Church at Princeton
University. Church also
developed a solution to
the decision problem:
lambda calculus

1938
Starts working on codes
for the British
government

1939
Recorded in transcripts of
visiting lecturers at
Cambridge disagreeing
with Ludwig Wittgenstein
about the foundation of
mathematics

1939
Reports to Bletchley Park
the day after war with
Germany is declared

1941
Proposes to Joan Clarke,
fellow mathematician,
but later calls it off

1948
Appointed reader in the
Mathematics Department
at Victoria University,
Manchester where he
works on the Manchester
Mark 1 computer

1950
Proposes what is now
known as the 'Turing
Test' to separate artificial
intelligence from humans

1952
Convicted for 'gross
indecency'. Turing's
solicitor does not defend
him

7 June 1954
Found dead by his cleaner
with a half-eaten apple,
speculated as being
where Turing put a fatal
dose of poison

ALAN TURING

The son of a civil servant, Turing's genius was recognized by his teachers as early as six, and he was an enthusiastic student. When he was prevented from getting to his boarding school at age 13 by a national strike, he cycled 97 km (60 miles) to attend.

While Turing was at Kings College, Cambridge, he became interested in a fashionable subject within mathematics: the question of whether the field had absolute foundations. A system that met these criteria needed to include an 'effective procedure' to test the truth of a mathematical statement. Before computer algorithms existed, Turing proposed a theoretical machine that could perform one instruction at a time based on a scanning head moving along an infinite strip of symbols, adding additional ones according to its instructions, then moving on in one direction or the next. This led Turing to the idea that the guidance itself could be programmed in, rather than building a machine for each task – a programmable computer.

After a stint at Princeton, where he met John von Neumann, he returned to Cambridge and, even before the Second World War, began working at the Government Code and Cypher School (the British code-breaking organization). During the war he adapted a Polish solution for decrypting the German Enigma code to create a more general solution (to overcome complexities the Germans were adding to the system). The first electromechanical computer was installed in Bletchley Park in 1940 and the system had a significant effect in reducing Allied losses, though Turing and others felt they could do more with greater resources – so much so they wrote directly to Winston Churchill. At Bletchley Park, Turing took a particular interest in the especially complicated naval Enigma code, for which Colossus – the first programable digital computer – was built to help address.

After the war, Turing moved first to Hampton, London, to work on the Automatic Computing Engine (ACE), then headed back to Cambridge and wrote a paper on intelligent machinery. At his next location, Manchester, he even began writing a chess-playing program.

In 1952 Turing was arrested for 'gross indecency' (at that time homosexuality was illegal in the UK). He opted for hormone treatment (chemical castration) rather than a custodial sentence, and it's believed this treatment led to Turing's death by suicide in 1954. He is thought to have put poison on an apple and bitten it, inspired by his favourite fairy tale. The UK government and the queen have made apologies and granted a posthumous pardon. Turing's name is given to the most prestigious award in the field he effectively created, computer science.

Adam Juniper

APPENDICES

RESOURCES

BOOKS

Code Simplicity: The Fundamentals of Software
Max Kanat-Alexander
(O'Reilly Media, 2012)

Introduction to Algorithms
Thomas H. Cormen, Charles E. Leiserson,
Ronald L. Rivest, Clifford Stein
(MIT Press, 2009)

*A Programmer's Guide to Computer Science:
A Virtual Degree for the Self-taught Developer*
Dr. William M. Springer II, Nicholas
R. Allgood, et al.
(Jaxson Media, 2019)

Structure & Interpretation of Computer Programs
Harold Abelson, Gerald Jay Sussman,
Julie Sussman
(MIT Press, 1996)

Turing's Vision: The Birth of Computer Science
Chris Bernhardt
(MIT Press, 2017)

WEBSITES

Codeacademy
codecademy.com
Free online coding classes.

Coursera
learntocodewith.me/coursera
Massive open online course provider with free courses in coding.

edX
edx.org
Massive open online course provider with free courses in coding.

freeCodeCamp
freecodecamp.org
Learn to code for free.

Swift Playgrounds
apple.com/swift/playgrounds
An interactive and fun app for learning the Swift programming language – no prior knowledge of coding required.

W3schools
w3schools.com
The world's largest web developer site – a free online resource with tutorials and reference materials on 14 programming languages.

PODCASTS

Automators
relay.fm/automators
David Sparks and Rosemary Orchard host a
podcast about automation.

List Envy
listenvypod.com/e/top-5-algorithms-that-
changed-the-world-37e55f75a54106/
The top 5 algorithms that changed the world.

NOTES ON CONTRIBUTORS

EDITOR

Mark Steadman is a coding entrepreneur who created Podiant.co, one of the world's leading podcasting platforms, from his apartment. It has received praise from *The Guardian* and *The Verge*, among others, and has even got a helpful robot (that he programmed)! His love of code is such that he hand-coded a personalized text adventure game as a Christmas present for his friends. When he's not bringing a digital project to life in code form, he's creating a new soundscape; his *Hitchhiker's Guide to the Galaxy* discussion podcast, *Beware of the Leopard*, has been aired on the BBC.

CONTRIBUTORS

Adam Juniper has spent much of his life carefully ducking between both sides of the war that is publishing. Sometimes he's hunkering down behind his keyboard carefully crafting the words which will help share his years of expertise (on subjects as diverse as drone programming or smart home planning). Other times he is to be found scouring the surface of the planet for creative talents who should be published; he specializes in creative projects such as the charity photography book *Covid Street*. Just because he's managed to persuade a few lines of code to act as simple robot butlers when it comes to turning lights on and off doesn't mean he needn't spend some time learning code from sprawling online resources. Oh, and since you've got this far, he's prepared to admit that when he's doing neither, you'll likely find him pretending to be emperor of the world in the game *Sid Meier's Civilization* or, since the virus took its hold, pretending to be a teacher!

Suze Shardlow wrote her first line of code as a small child in 1982 and started making websites in 1996. She is an accomplished technical writer, coding instructor and public speaker. A familiar face on the tech conference scene, Suze MCs and gives talks at local and global industry events. Suze teaches coding in the UK and overseas and has designed and delivered public speaking workshops for women in tech around the world. She is passionate about demystifying tech for international audiences through her blog; she also hosts an educational YouTube series interviewing women about tech roles and career progression. Suze's leadership experience includes directing two of the largest software developer groups in London, with over 10000 members. Her work has been cited in academic papers and at major global conferences, while her community event methodologies have been replicated by tech organizations in Silicon Valley, California. Suze is a multiple award winner and is on the Women in Software Power List. Outside of tech, Suze competes in 5km and 10km races and is a keen crafter. You can find Suze online at https://suze.dev

INDEX

ACKNOWLEDGMENTS

The publisher would like to thank the following for permission to reproduce copyright material:

Alamy/Photo 12: 17; Science History Images: 17; Mint Images Limited: 17; GL Archive: 25; Prisma by Dukas Presseagentur GmbH: 25; Lenscap: 27; Alpha Historica: 27; Nick Higham: 29; INTERFOTO: 33; Aflo Co Ltd: 33; Science History Images: 33, 43; Granger Historical Picture Archive: 44; Michael Betteridge: 47; Stephen Barnes/Techonology: 47; INTEROFOTO: 47; Retro Ark: 47; Science History Images: 47; The Book Worm: 47; agefotostock: 61; DWD-Media: 67; PictureLux/ The Hollywood Archive: 67; Robert Clay: 74; Konstantin Savusia: 79; RGB Ventures/SuperStock: 90; Westend GmbH: 95; UPI: 132; Robert Hoetink: 145; Alpha Historica: 150

Getty Images/Sepia Times and Universal Images Group: 15; IanDagnall Computing: 18; Hulton Archive: 23; Bettmann: 23; Amanda Lucier/For The Washington Post: 64; Bettmann: 115, 145

NASA: 21

New York Public Library: 23

Shutterstock/Rolling Orange: 15; Morphart Creation: 15; nontthepcool: 17; Natbasil: 17; Antony Robinson: 23; eans: 25; Aaren Goldin: 27; PhilipYb Studio: 29; Maxx-Studio: 31; golfyinterlude: 31; Przemek Iciak: 31; Kasefoto: 31; Anna Molcharenko: 31; Everett Collection: 31; Christos Georgiou: 31; Dragance 137: 31; Bernulius: 33; Cristian Storto: 33; Everett Collection: 33; Fouad A. Saad: 33; Everett Collection: 35; Sacho Films: 35; Dr Project: 35; marekuliasz: 43; ConceptCafe: 43; nicemonkey: 43; Alexander Kirch: 47; Roman Belogorodov: 47; Uliya Krakos: 47; Alika-Dream: 47; Vivi-o: 49; Everett Collection: 49; Molotok289: 49; iadams: 49; derGriza: 49; Nattanon Tavonthammarit: 51; Rebius: 51; Markus Mainka: 51; Rashevskyi Viacheslav: 51; Joachim Wendler: 51; Number1411: 51; AlexY38: 51; Przemyslaw Szablowski: 51; Andrii Stepaniuk: 51; tele52: 51; Amguy: 61; BoxerX: 61; Ilaya Studio: 61; Yulia Reznikov: 63; Angyalosi Beata: 63; Elena Schweitzer: 63; Aksenenko Olga: 63; Stephen VanHorn: 63; Everett Collection: 67; Martin Bergsma: 67; Dan Kosmeyer: 67; Ainul muttaqin: 67; Pro Symbols: 67; Everett Collection: 69; Triff: 69; Romeo168: 69; Jojje: 69; Everett Collection: 71; Studio_G: 71; Swill Klitch: 71; Komleva: 71; Neil Carrington: 73; Everett Collection: 73; Andy Dean Photography: 73; Ulrich Mueller: 73; goodcat: 73; rangizzz: 73; Kostenyukova Nataliya: 73; Makstorm: 73; vinap: 73; sondem: 77; Xavier Gallego morell: 77; FabrikaSimf: 77; Everett Collection: 77; INGARA: 77; WNGSTD: 77; Sorapop Udomsri: 79; kathayut kongmanee: 79; Axro: 79; Africa Studio: 79; SpicyTruffel: 79; urfin: 81; Hurst Photo: 81; BiggsJee: 81; Natee Photo: 81; anna

k: 81; Carlos Amarillo: 81; varuna: 81; bqmeng: 81; Everett Collection: 81; kasakphoto: 83; Rawpixel.com: 83; Gorodenkoff: 83; Artfurt: 83; Kamenetskiy Konstantin: 89; sondem: 89; nicemonkey: 89; Stock Rocket: 89; MicroOne: 89; naskami: 89; Technisorn Stocker: 89; Butus: 93; artjazz: 93; Emiliya Hva: 93; ilallali: 93; Standard Studio: 93; Everett Collection: 93; Odua Images: 93; Dalibor Zivotic: 97; sagir: 97; Everett Collection: 97; Demianstur: 97; Jane Kelly: 97; Paolo Bona: 101; iceink: 103; Protosov AN: 105; Everett Collection: 105; Terekhov Igor: 105; simone vancini: 105; 3DDock: 107; ZHU JIAN ZHONG: 107; VectorPixelStar: 107; Macrovector: 107; RHJPhotoandilustration: 115; Filipchuk Maksym: 115; Alena Ohneva: 115; Kasefoto: 117; industryviews: 117; Kovalov Anatolii: 117; Marti Bug Catcher: 119; Everett Collection: 119; Topconcept: 121; Oleg Shakirov: 121; Everett Collection: 121; Morphart Creation: 123; BGStock72: 125; Everett Collection: 139; bumbumbo: 141

Wikimedia Commons: 15, 23, 25, 27, 29, 43, 49, 93, 99, 101, 103, 113, 115, 119, 123, 125, 127, 129, 131, 139, 141, 143, 145, 147, 149

All reasonable efforts have been made to trace copyright holders and to obtain their permission for the use of copyright material. The publisher apologizes for any errors or omissions in the list above and will gratefully incorporate any corrections in future reprints if notified.